Marketing of Consumer Financial Products

Marketing of Consumer Financial Products

Insights From Service Marketing

Ritu Srivastava

BEP

BUSINESS EXPERT PRESS

Leader in applied, concise business books

First published in 2023 by
Business Expert Press, LLC
222 East 46th Street, New York, NY 10017
www.businessexpertpress.com

ISBN-13: 978-1-63742-430-8 (paperback)
ISBN-13: 978-1-63742-431-5 (e-book)

Business Expert Press Marketing Collection

First edition: 2023

10 9 8 7 6 5 4 3 2 1

Description

Banking and Financial Services is an important pillar of any national economy. Across countries this industry has now become competitive. While they were earlier dealt with a welfare orientation, the competition has pressed this sector to turn to the "Marketing" discipline that can help in creating distinctive competitive advantages for the financial companies.

Marketing has been traditionally goods oriented with a business-to-customer focus. However, it is established that service organizations also need a focused marketing strategy in the business-to-consumer space. Financial service products can be classified as service products and this is the starting point for this book. While there are books available on Financial Services Marketing, there is none available with a service marketing perspective. As soon as organizations start looking at their financial products as service products, they would start identifying that apart from working on technical features for product augmentation. There is a scope and need for innovating and improving the service-related characteristics of the core product as well as associated services.

The book starts by giving an overview of different individual-related financial products in Chapter 1. The reader is smoothly shifted to the service-related characteristics of such products while building the need for a marketing strategy. This is where certain unique service marketing concepts are introduced apart from the need and ways of doing personal financial planning. The unique aspect of this book is that this deals with both the sides of business that is, the firm and the customer, and considers their needs and concerns while building the marketing strategy.

Chapter 2 deals with the consumer decision-making process and the critical points that need to be taken care of by the financial organizations. It introduces the concepts of service encounter, service script, and service blueprint to manage satisfactory firm customer interaction for a financial company. The role of culture and how to deal with misbehaving customers also has been dealt with in detail in this chapter. The author introduces a framework for customer satisfaction in the purchase journey in this chapter, which is based out of field research.

Chapter 3 discusses the role of customer expectations and the need to understand them as financial service providers. The chapter talks of how financial companies need to set and manage customer expectations, which will help the firm in meeting them satisfactorily. The role of physical settings and ambience is also explained through the concept of servicescapes. Chapter 4 follows the concept of service quality and how expectations as dealt in Chapter 3 need to be mapped with customer perceptions of service, service quality, and customer satisfaction through the Gaps model of service quality. Chapter 5 highlights steps to implement a relationship-oriented retail marketing strategy in financial service organizations through a research study, which could create competitive advantage for the financial organization.

This book uses insights from services marketing to illustrate how financial service providers should utilize service marketing concepts to provide customers with quality, satisfaction, and memorable experience. This book is particularly useful to managers in financial organizations, executives enrolled in a management course, and faculty and postgraduate students of a management course to get a detailed overview of financial products and working out a marketing strategy, which is customer oriented with a service marketing application in a crisp and concise manner. This book is also useful for general readers who would be consumers to financial organization in various ways and can understand the need to do financial planning while getting some idea about the financial companies as well.

Keywords

financial service products; relationship marketing; service approach; customer centric; financial customers

Contents

Chapter 1   An Overview of Consumer Financial Products and Service-Oriented Marketing 1

Chapter 2   Distinctive Features of Retail Financial Products as Services and Consumer Decision Making 33

Chapter 3   Managing Customer Expectations 59

Chapter 4   Customer Perceptions of Financial Service Products, Service Quality, and Customer Satisfaction.....................83

Chapter 5   Implementing a Relationship-Oriented Service Plan for a Financial Service Product...99

References...103

Appendix 1 *Financial Goals Worksheet*...109

Appendix 2 *Customer Service Sample Voice Prompts for Banks and Related Financial Services*..111

Appendix 3 *When Serving Customers Became Tough?*.........................119

About the Author..127

Index 129

CHAPTER 1

An Overview of Consumer Financial Products and Service-Oriented Marketing

Chapter Overview

This chapter details about various types of financial products and their role in the economy, to help the reader understand the whole gamut of financial products. Taking the customer perspective, the chapter then moves to the process of individual financial planning process and how financial organizations need to understand it through the consumer's perspective. The chapter concludes by presenting a marketing strategy framework for financial organizations and highlighting the augmentation of such products for the growth of the company.

The Role of Retail Financial Products in a Country's Economy

The financial system of a country is made up of different kinds of financial institutions, markets, instruments, claims, liabilities, transactions, and so on. The system of finance of a country contributes to economic development by promoting wealth creation through the association of investments with savings. The financial system promotes the fund flow of household as savings to business firms as investors and thus helps in the development of both through wealth creation. Thus, the characteristic features of the financial systems are:

- It connects investors and savers;
- It stimulates both investments and savings;

- It aids in capital formation;
- It aids in risk allocation;
- It enables financial markets' expansion.

Financial Markets

These are exchanges where buyers and sellers trade financial assets such as currencies, bonds, stocks, and other instruments. Money and capital markets make up a financial market. The capital market trades long-term assets with a maturity of more than a year, while the money market trades short-term instruments with a maturity of less than a year.

Financial Institutions

These are the mediators of financial markets that conduct financial transactions. It can be a money making or not-for-profit organization that fetches money from individuals and diverts into financial assets such as loans, deposits, bonds, and stocks. There are two types of financial institutions. The first ones are called banking institutions that can collect money from individuals and provide interests on deposits. The money collected is used to give loans at an interest to financial customers. The second kind of financial institutions are nonbanking ones that include insurance companies, mutual funds, and brokerage firms. These institutions do not collect deposits or provide loans to public; rather they offer financial products that can be sold to financial customers. Financial institutions also cover regulatory organizations, which take care of investors' interests, intermediaries such as banks and so on, that provide financial products including short-term loans to individual customers and nonmediators that provide long-term corporate loans (Figure 1.1).

Fiduciary Responsibility

Banking and other financial services have a fiduciary duty to act on behalf of another person or persons, prioritizing their clients' interests over their own, and maintaining good faith and trust. Financial firms must be legally and ethically bound to act in their clients' best interests as fiduciaries. This is an important aspect of the management of such a company.

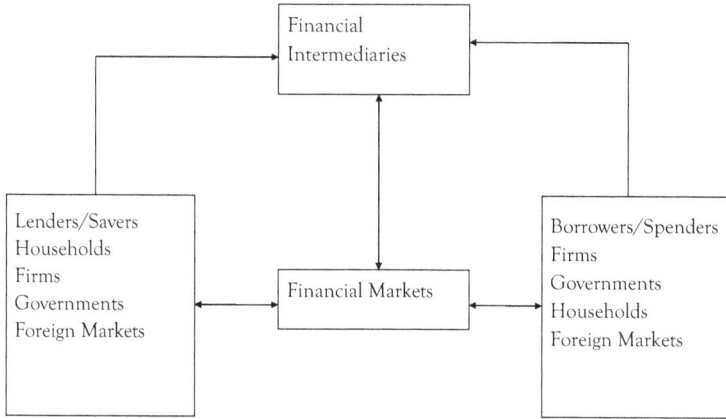

Figure 1.1 The financial system

Source: Adapted from Mishkin (2007).

Commercial Banks

Commercial banks are a sort of financial institution that receives deposits from the general public and disburses loans to encourage consumption and investment in the hopes of making a profit. The term "commercial bank" can also refer to a bank, or a division of a big bank, that interacts with corporate organizations/corporations or mid-sized firms, as a distinction between retail and investment banks. Commercial banks can be private- or public-sector organizations.

Commercial banks' wide responsibility is to deliver financial services to individuals and corporations in order to ensure long-term economic prosperity and social stability. As a result, commercial banks' primary purpose is credit generation. Commercial banks have the following primary goals:

1. To take various types of deposits from the general population (i.e., from its customers). Savings accounts, recurring accounts, and fixed deposits are examples of these. On request or after a set period of time, these deposits are returned to the customer.
2. To supply various types of advances and loans, overdraft, cash credit, bill discounting, and money at call are just a few examples. They also provide term and demand loans to a wide range of customers who

have enough collateral. Commercial banks function as trustees for their clients' wills and other documents.

3. Credit is established through the use of a credit and payment intermediary. Deposits are absorbed by commercial banks, which are subsequently used to provide loans. Based on check circulation and transfer settlement, the loans are turned into derivative deposits. To some extent, derivative funds that are many times the original deposits are higher than they were previously, greatly enhancing commercial banks' ability to serve economic development.

All the commercial banks have to follow the regulations set by the regulatory authority of a particular country, for example, in India, it is the Reserve Bank of India (RBI). The Indian commercial banks have to follow a number of conditions like holding bank reserves and keeping a minimum amount of capital. As already mentioned, the commercial banks give a number of services as products. These include banking's main services, such as loans and deposits, as well as various services related to financial services and payment systems. As a result, commercial banks provide the following services:

- Acceptance of money on a variety of deposit accounts;
- Borrowing money through an overdraft;
- Offering both unsecured and secured loans;
- Transaction accounts are available;
- Treasury and cash management;
- Private equity funding;
- Issuance of bank checks and drafts;
- Internet banking, electronic funds transfer at point of sale, telegraphic transfer, and other payment methods.

In addition to these services, the commercial banks also offer some secondary services that can be separated as utility and agency functions. The agency functions comprise:

- Clearance and collection of checks, interest warrant, and dividends;

- Assist in the payment of rent, insurance premiums, and other expenses;
- Foreign exchange transactions;
- Selling and purchasing stocks;
- Acting as trustee, attorney, correspondent, and executor;
- Tax returns and revenues are accepted.

The utility purpose consists of:

- Provision of safe to customers;
- Money transferring facility;
- Issuance of traveler's checks;
- Acting as a referee;
- Payment of bills like phone, gas, water, and so on;
- Provision of cards as debit and credit.

Insurance Companies

Insurance is a means for savings or a protection against financial loss. It assists individuals in managing risk, primarily, the risk of a loss that is uncertain or conditional. The individual or organization (could be an insurance service provider, an underwriter, or an insurance carrier) that offers insurance plans is called the insurer and the one who/which buys insurance is called the insured or a policyholder. An insured gets a cover in the situation of a loss by paying certain amount of money to the insurer in the form of small payments, known as a premium, over a time and in case of loss, the insurer promises to pay damages for the loss. There could be monetary or nonmonetary loss; however, in nonmonetary, it has to be translated into monetary terms. An insured's insurable interest is frequently demonstrated through ownership, possession, or a prior relationship. A contract known as an insurance policy is issued to the insured entity. An insurance policy includes details regarding the terms and conditions under which the insurer agrees to pay a certain amount promised to the insured. In some situations, for example, in case, the risk is too big to insure, a primary insurer may bypass the risk by opting in for reinsurance. In reinsurance, another insurance service provider agrees to cover some risks.

Insurance services are based on the principle of gathering finances from various policyholders to reimburse for the losses that some insured may experience. In other words, the policyholders are safeguarded from losses for a specific sum of money. The amount money of premium is contingent upon the rate of occurrence and intensity of the event/situation.

There are seven common characteristics of a risk that can be insured by private organizations:

1. A big number of similar exposure units: Because insurance services rely on a group of policyholders collecting funds, insurers can take advantage of the law of large numbers, which asserts that expected losses equal actual losses.

2. Definite loss: This form of loss happens at a specific time and place, as well as the result of a known cause. The death of an insured individual under a life insurance policy is the most common occurrence. Automobile accidents, fires, and work-related injuries may all fall into this group.

3. Accidental loss: The occurrence that leads to a claim should be unforeseen, or at the very minimum beyond the insurance receiver's competence. The loss must be pure, that is, it must be the result of an event for which there is just a cost potential.

4. Large loss: For the insured, the size of the damage must be substantial. Premiums must cover both the expected cost of losses and the policy's administrative costs, such as loss adjustment and providing the capital required to assure that the insurer can pay claims.

5. Affordable premium: Even if insurance is available, it is unlikely to be purchased if the likelihood of an insured occurrence is so high, or the cost of the event is so high, that the resulting premium is too expensive in relation to the amount of protection provided.

6. Calculable loss: The likelihood of loss and the associated cost are two points that must be at least evaluated if not adequately calculated. The cost is related more to the capability of a normal human being in ownership of the insurance policy, whereas the likelihood of loss is more of a practical exercise. This must be supported with evidence of loss related to a claim filed under that policy so that a sufficient, specific, and objective assessment of the amount of damage recoverable as a consequence of the claim can be made.

7. Limited risk of catastrophically large losses: Insurable losses should be independent and noncatastrophic, which means they don't come all at once and unit losses aren't severe enough to throw the insurer out of business. Insurance companies may choose to limit their coverage to a single incident resulting in a small loss of capital.

Legal Requirements in Insurance

There are some legal requirements that need to be met while insuring an individual by insurance service provider. They are:

- Indemnity: The insurer only pays the insured up to the policyholder's interest in the event of specific losses.
- Benefit insurance: The insurance company has no recourse against the person who caused the accident. Even if the policyholder has already filed a lawsuit against the party that caused the accident for damages, the insurer is still obligated to compensate the insured.
- Insurable interest: The person insured must be straightly impacted by the loss and have a financial interest in it. Property or a person's insurable interests are both examples of insurable interest.
- Utmost good faith: The insurer and the insured are held together by the highest level of good faith. All significant facts should be disclosed by the insured.
- Contribution: Insurers with similar obligations contribute to the insured through a specific manner of indemnification.
- Subrogation: Insurance companies have legal authority to follow recoveries on behalf of their customers.
- Causa proxima, or proximate cause: The reason of loss should be incorporated in the insurance policy contract, as well as the primary cause of loss.
- Mitigation: In the event of a loss, the asset owner must attempt to mitigate the loss as much as possible in a manner comparable to how the asset would have been if it had not been insured.

Indemnification Concept in Insurance

To "indemnify" means to pay for a loss. This means to restore the insured to the state, to the best possible, prior to the occurrence of a particular incident or hazard. Therefore, insurance is normally regarded as a "contingent" insurance (i.e., in the occurrence of a stated event, an assertion is made) and not "indemnity" insurance. Insurance contracts that try to indemnify a policyholder are categorized into three:

- A "reimbursement" policy
- A "pay on behalf" or "on behalf of policy"
- An "indemnification" policy

For the insured, the result is usually the same: the insurer pays the loss and claims expenses.

- With a "reimbursement" policy, the insured may have to pay for a loss before being "reimbursed" by the insurance provider company and out-of-pocket costs, which may include claim fees with the insurer's permission.
- A "pay on behalf" policy means that the insurance company will support and compensate a claim on behalf of the policyholder, who will not have to pay anything out of pocket. Liability insurances are now written in "pay on behalf" terminology, which makes it easier for the insurance company to manage and control the claim.
- Under a "indemnification" policy, the insurance provider could generally "reimburse" or "pay on behalf of" it and the policyholder in the claim settlement process, whichever is best beneficial to it and the policyholder.

An entity (any kind of organization, an individual, a business, etc.) can give over the risk and become the "insured" as soon as the risk is managed by an "insurer." This is accomplished through the use of an insurance policy, which is a contract. The following are the components of an insurance contract:

- Participants' acknowledgment (insurer, insured, and benefi-ciaries);
- The precise loss event covered;
- The coverage period;
- The coverage amount (i.e., the amount paid to the policy-holder or beneficiary in the case of a loss) and the premium;
- Exclusions (events that aren't protected).

An insured is thus called as "indemnified" against the losses covered in the policy.

The coverage allows the policyholder to file a claim with the insurer for the insured amount of damage as specified in the policy when the protected parties experience a loss as a result of a specified risk. The premium is the amount paid by the insured to the insurer as compensation for risk estimation. Premiums from a number of policyholders are used to fund accounts set aside for claim payment—in theory for a small number of claimants—and administration costs. The residual margin is an insurer's profit until it has enough money set aside to cover any losses (called reserves).

An insurance policy may have a number of exclusions. Exclusions in an insurance contract emphasize on the clauses that signify what is not included. Policies typically comprise a number of exclusions.

Social Effects of Insurance

As the cost of losses and damage shifts, insurance may have a number of societal implications. It has the potential to increase fraud while also assisting individuals and society in preparing for disasters and alleviating the disastrous repercussions on both a familial and societal level.

Insurance can influence the possibility of losses due to insurance fraud, moral hazard, and insurance service providers' preventive activities. According to insurance experts, moral hazard refers to increased risk as a result of unintentional negligence, whereas insurance fraud refers to increased risk as a result of deliberate carelessness or indifference. Insurers utilize a variety of methods to counteract neglect, including checks, policy limits requiring specified forms of maintenance, and possible reductions for loss justification efforts. Although insurers may theoretically incentivize investment in loss reduction, some experts have suggested that in the past, insurers have been hesitant to implement loss control measures—particularly to avoid catastrophe losses such as typhoons—due to concerns about rate decreases and legal wranglings. Nonetheless, insurers have become increasingly active in loss reduction from around 1996.

Nonbanking Financial Companies

A nonbanking financial institution (NBFI) or nonbank financial company (NBFC) is a financial institution that is not regulated by a national or international banking regulator and does not have a full banking license. NBFCs provide banking-related financial services such as contractual savings, risk pooling, investing, and market brokering. Money exchanges, pawn shops, insurance agencies, check cashing outlets, cashier's check issuers, payday lending, and microloan organizations are examples of such institutions. The significance of NBFIs in supporting an economy has been recognized, since they provide many substitutes to convert an economy's reserves into capital investment that operate as supporting facilities should the main form of intermediation fail. Operations of NBFIs many times classify in the banking rules of a country.

NBFI's Role in Financial System

NBFIs supplement banks by arranging for excess resources to be allocated to persons and businesses in need. NBFIs also encourage competition in the provision of financial services. NBFIs unbundle and customize financial services to match the needs of individual customers, whereas banks may offer a packaged set of financial services. Furthermore, different NBFIs may specialize in a specific field and obtain a competitive advantage in terms of information. By unbundling, targeting, and specializing procedures, NBFIs promote competition in the financial services sector. NBFCs offer a wide range of banking services, including retirement planning, private education funding, credit and lending facilities, and much more. Trading in money markets, underwriting stocks and shares, and other liabilities are all examples of term finance certificates (TFCs).

These companies also include wealth management services such as stock and share collections, discounting services such as instrument discounting, and merger and acquisition consulting. The nonbanking financial enterprises have increased dramatically in number in recent years, as retail and industrial companies, as well as venture capital firms, have entered the lending market. Nonbank institutions frequently assist enterprises with property investments and market or industry feasibility studies. Because they are not permitted to accept deposits from the general public, companies must find alternative sources of funding, such as issuing debt securities. Checks, savings accounts, and current accounts are not available from NBFCs. Fixed or time deposits are the only ones that are accepted.

NBFIs Facilitate Growth

Some research has found a positive link between financial development and economic growth. In general, NBFIs in a market-based financial system are more sophisticated than those in a bank-based financial system, which is beneficial to banker–broker economic growth ties.

NBFIs Promote Stability

As part of a multidimensional financial system, NBFCs can insulate economies against financial shocks and allow for speedy recovery when they occur. However, the financial system's susceptibility may be exacerbated by the lack of proper fiscal norms for NBFIs. The shadow banking system that these organizations have built could be unstable because not all NBFIs are well regulated. Hedge funds and structured investment vehicles, in particular, were items that drew NBFI attention away from pension funds and insurance businesses until the global financial crisis of 2007–2008, but were mostly disregarded by policy watchdogs. Because these NBFIs lack a banking license, they are usually unregulated by government authorities and credit reporting agencies in a number of nations. As a result, if NBFIs control a considerable portion of overall financial assets, the entire financial system could be disrupted. Owing to a lack of NBFI regulation, the 1997 Asian financial crisis was exacerbated by a lending bubble and asset overheating. The Asian financial crisis of 1997 was precipitated when asset values fell and loan defaults increased, leaving most of Southeast Asia and Japan with depreciated currencies and growing private debt.

Owing to increased competition, established lenders are reticent to incorporate NBFIs in current credit-information-sharing arrangements. In addition, the majority of NBFIs lack the technological skills required to participate in information sharing networks. In comparison to banks, NBFIs provide less information to credit reporting agencies on average. To ensure their continuous growth and existence while maintaining their innovativeness, NBFCs must be regulated. Creating a regulatory sandbox in a varied environment will help them achieve their goals. The regulatory sandbox has been adopted by several countries, and many more will do so in the near future.

Mutual Funds, Pension Funds, and Cooperatives

A mutual fund is a corporation that collects money from multiple investors and invests it in stocks, bonds, and short-term loans. The portfolio of a mutual fund is made up of all of the fund's holdings. Mutual funds are purchased by investors. Each share represents an investor's portion of the fund's ownership and revenue. Mutual funds are a popular investment option because they often provide the following benefits:

- **Management on a professional level**: The research is done for you by the fund managers. They choose the securities and keep track of their performance.
- **Diversification of risk**: "Don't put all your eggs in one basket," as the saying goes. Mutual funds usually invest in a variety of businesses and industries. This reduces your risk if one of your companies fails.
- **Affordability**: The initial investment and future purchases for most mutual funds are fixed at a low dollar sum.
- **Liquidity**: Investors in mutual funds can simply redeem their shares for the current net asset value (NAV) plus any redemption costs at any time.

Money market funds, bond funds, stock funds, and target date funds are the four primary types of mutual funds. Each variety has its own set of characteristics, hazards, and benefits.

Types of Mutual Funds

i. Money market funds have a low-risk profile. They are only allowed to invest in specific high-quality, short-term investments issued by U.S. firms, as well as federal, state, and local governments, by law.

ii. Bond funds are riskier than money market funds because they are designed to generate bigger returns. Bond funds' risks and rewards can vary considerably because of the many different types of bonds available.

iii. Corporate stocks are the focus of stock funds. Stock funds aren't all created equal. Here are a few examples:
   - Growth funds invest in stocks that don't pay a monthly dividend but have the potential to outperform the market.
   - Dividend-paying equities are the focus of income funds.
   - Index funds follow a certain market index, such as the S&P 500 Index.
   - Sector funds are focused on a specific industry segment.

iv. Target date funds invest in a variety of stocks, bonds, and other assets. According to the fund's strategy, the mix steadily varies over time. Target date funds, often known as lifecycle funds, are created for people who know when they want to retire.

Benefits and Risks of Mutual Funds

Mutual funds provide competent investment management as well as the possibility of diversification. They also provide three other ways to make money:

- Payments of dividends: Dividends on stocks and interest on bonds can both provide income to a fund. The fund then distributes nearly all of the revenue to the shareholders, less expenditures.

- Distributions of capital gains: The value of a fund's securities may rise in value. A capital gain occurs when a fund sells an investment that has gained in value. The fund distributes these capital gains, minus any capital losses, to investors at the end of the year.
- Rise of NAV: After deducting expenses, the market value of a fund's portfolio improves, which enhances the value of the fund and its shares. The higher the NAV, the more valuable your investment is.

Every fund entails some level of risk. Because the securities held by mutual funds might lose value, you could lose some or all of your money if you invest in them. As market circumstances change, dividends or interest payments may also alter.

Because previous performance does not indicate future returns, the past performance of a fund is not as essential as you may assume. Past performance, on the other hand, can tell you how volatile or stable a fund has been over time. The larger the investment risk, the more volatile the fund.

Buying and Selling of Mutual Funds

Rather than buying from other investors, investors purchase mutual fund shares directly from the fund or through a fund broker. The fund's per share NAV plus any fees payable at the time of purchase, such as sales loads, is the price that investors pay for the mutual fund.

Shares in mutual funds are "redeemable," which means that investors can sell them back to the fund at any time. In most cases, the fund is required to provide you the payment within seven days. The prospectus has to be read carefully before investing in a mutual fund. The prospectus provides details of the mutual fund's investing goals, risks, performance, and costs.

A mutual fund, like any other business, has expenses. Fees and expenditures are used by funds to pass on these costs to investors. Fees and expenditures differ from one fund to the next. To achieve the same returns for you, a high-cost fund must outperform a low-cost fund. Even minor changes in fees can result in significant profits over time. There are free mutual fund cost calculators online that will help you figure out how the costs of various mutual funds stack up over time and eat into your returns.

Pension Fund

Any plan, fund, or scheme that provides retirement income is referred to as a pension fund, also known as a superannuation fund in some countries. Pension funds are a collection of monetary contributions from pension plans established by businesses, unions, or other organizations to pay for the retirement benefits of their employees or members. In most countries, pension funds are the largest investment blocks, and they control the stock markets where they invest. They, along with insurance companies and investment trusts, make up the institutional investor sector when handled by professional fund managers. Pension funds are typically excluded from capital gains tax, and earnings on their investment portfolios are either tax-deferred or tax-free.

Cooperatives: A cooperative is a member-owned organization designed to meet the members' social, economic, and cultural requirements. Regardless of the number of shares they own or the position they hold in the cooperative, each member has equal voting rights. The members, directors, and workers of a cooperative are not accountable for the entity's debts because the cooperative is a separate legal entity.

Psychology of Money

When we talk about financial products, the central product is money and money comes with a psychological legacy in every individual. There is a heavy emotional connection between an individual and his/her attitude toward money. It thus becomes very important for financial institutions to hit at the right emotional chord of the individual customer. Financial institutions do develop typologies of its different customers. One such typology is based on an individual's attitude and behavior toward financial matters on the basis of the following listed variables:

- Control over spending and saving;
- An interest in and understanding of finances;

- A desire to save rather than spend; and
- Confidence in or a need for advice.

Similarly there have been typologies related to investor psychology:

- Market follower versus contrarian;
- Risk tolerance levels;
- Saving and spending habits.

The saving and spending typologies date back to Sigmund Freud's period. He distinguished between obsessive and noncompulsive spenders, as well as subtypes such as pretended wealthy and pretended poverty. Modern psychologists expanded on this by coining terms such as "fanatical consumers," "passive customers," and "esteem buyers." The psychology of spending is of particular interest to the marketers of debt products. They seek prospects that create and build balances while also continuously paying them off gradually. It has been noticed that there is a fine line between defaulting overspenders and nonoverspenders.

Individual Financial Planning

While understanding financial consumer products, it becomes important to start looking at these products from the customer perspective. Largely, the available text is from an organization perspective. The best way to start developing this understanding is to start looking at what are the sources of funds for an individual and where does he spend. Similarly what are his/her saving and investing options? After these two concerns have been looked at, income, age, and family life cycle stage have to be considered to accommodate the differences. We would start understanding the individual and developing the customer perspective from now on. This section details about the individual financial planning process and how different customers need to adapt as per their needs. The practice of planning and managing different personal financial activities is called as personal finance or individual finance. These activities comprise generating income, saving expending, capitalizing, and protecting. The procedure of organizing personal finance can be briefed in a

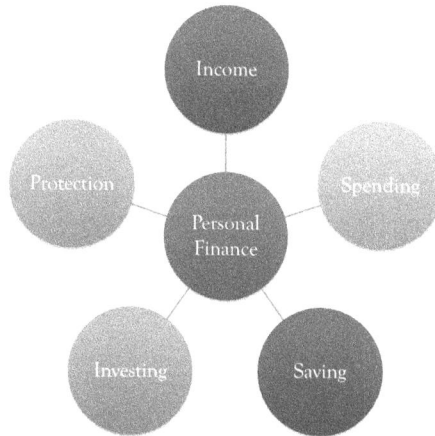

Figure 1.2 Areas of individual financial planning

budget, also called the financial plan. Figure 1.2 depicts the areas of individual financial planning.

Income

Income denotes the cash inflow sources of an individual. This is used to maintain self and his/her family. This is where personal financial planning process starts. Income can come from various sources such as:

- Salaries
- Pensions
- Bonuses
- Wages
- Dividends

All the above-mentioned income sources make money, which can be used by an individual to spend, save, or invest.

Spending

This head includes all the expenses that an individual incurs for purchasing goods and services or everything that is for consumption and not for investment. Spending can be classified into two categories, that is, cash (paying via money in hand) and credit (paying by borrowing money). The common sources of spending are:

- Rent and fees
- Food
- Taxes and duties
- Credit card payments
- Mortgage payments
- Travel
- Entertainment

The greater part of an individual's income is allotted to spending. The expenses reduce the amount of cash that is available to an individual for saving and capitalizing. If expenditure is more than the income, the person has a shortage. It is imperative to manage both pay and expenses. People exercise greater control over discretionary expenses rather than the income. For managing individual finance, there is a need of developing good spending habits.

Saving

Saving includes the excess cash that is retained in the income after accounting for expenses. The saved money can be used for future investment or spending. Depending on the expenses, if there is a surplus between the earning and the spending and keeping some liquid money (which can be easily withdrawn/made available) as savings, the income that is left can be used for investment or any other discretionary spending, which is kept aside for future expenditure or investments. Managing savings is an important dimension of individual financial planning. Savings have different forms, the popular ones are:

- Hard cash
- Savings account in banks
- Checking account in banks
- Money market securities

People typically save to maintain their cash flow and close the short-term gap between their salary and expenditures. Excessive savings, on the other hand, may not be regarded wise because it yields little or no return when compared to investing.

Investing

Investing is about the purchase of assets, which would fetch a rate of return. When an individual invests money, he/she expects that with time more money will be received than what was invested. There is risk involved in the investment activity. The financial products available in the market in which the individual invests have different types of benefits and risks associated. Thus not all assets may lead to producing a positive rate of return. It is here that decisions need expertise and thorough understanding of that particular asset along with the understanding of the connection between risk and return. The usual methods of investing include:

- Stocks
- Mutual funds
- Bonds
- Private companies
- Real estate
- Art
- Commodities

Because of the complexity involved in the investment decision people need professional advice. This book may serve as a reference to people who are trying to understand the basics of the financial products at an individual level, executives who need to build on their expertise in a crisp manner from the customer perspective and not the company perspective, and management students who are trying to understand this decision and the multiple perspectives involved. The big differences between risk and reward among different investments are explained in the preceding section, which forms an important segment of the personal financial plan.

Protection

Personal financial protection is a broad term that refers to a variety of products that can be used to safeguard against an unexpected and unpleasant incident. The following are some of the most commonly used protective products:

- Life insurance
- Health insurance
- Estate planning

Apart from understanding the benefits and advantages of each type of product, an individual needs to decide between investment, protection, and savings. The financial products are technically different from consumable physical goods. Apart from them being a service product, the terms and conditions involved in them are not very easily understood. Thus people need professional advice in these products also. There is an entire sequence of analysis that needs to be done to correctly assess an individual's insurance and estate planning needs.

The Individual Financial Planning Process Illustrated

Having a well-established financial plan, which is followed strictly, is at the root of good financial management. The five areas of income, expenditure, savings, investment, and protection are wrapped in a financial plan or budget. Professional financial advisers and agents from the financial products companies (banks, mutual funds, and insurance) give their expert services to individuals to build their portfolios by understanding their requirements and objectives and developing an apt strategy.

The key steps of the financial planning procedure are as follows.

1. Evaluation of Income and Managing the Money

In the first step, the individual has to assess the income from different sources. We can illustrate this through the example of Rajesh. Rajesh is a 24-year-old young man who has just got his engineering degree and would be starting with his first salaried job. He has been placed in a multinational corporation at an annual package of US$ 10,000. Salary is his only source of income. He is not married, so does not have any other expenses except for managing his own regular expenses of food, shelter, clothes, and so on. His parents live in Ranchi and he is based in Gurugram, Haryana, India. Being a corporate hub, the cost of living in Gurugram is 44.21 percent higher than in Ranchi.[1] To build a financial plan for Rajesh once he is sure of his income, next he has to set the financial planning goals for himself. If he has the knowledge and tools he can do it himself, otherwise he may need to get professional advice or he may even consult some online free tools available.

2. Goals

To set financial goals there is a need to look not only short term but also long term. Maslow's Need Hierarchy Theory of Motivation explains how human needs are classified into five levels, which progress by satisfying the lower order need to move to the next levels. The following Figure 1.3 highlights the hierarchy of needs with reference to the financial needs of an individual.

At the basic needs level, an individual has to look for income that would cover his physiological needs to survive such as food, housing, and daily expenses. For Rajesh, 10 percent of his present income suffices for the physiological need. Once the basic needs are covered an individual must start planning for his financial safety, which is covered under the expense head "protection." This would cover insurance including life and health. Since Rajesh is still a bachelor, he decides to invest 25 percent of his income here. There is also a need to create an emergency fund to help prepare for unforeseen events and risks. Rajesh being single decided to keep 30 percent of his income for emergency funds. Ideally, the emergency fund must cover three months of living expenses. This could also be a part of the expense head "savings." He also had an idea that he may get married by the age of 30, by then he would have substantial safety bucket

---

[1] www.numbeo.com/cost-of-living/compare_cities.jsp?country1=India&country2=India&city1=Ranchi&city2=Gurgaon&tracking=getDispatchComparison.

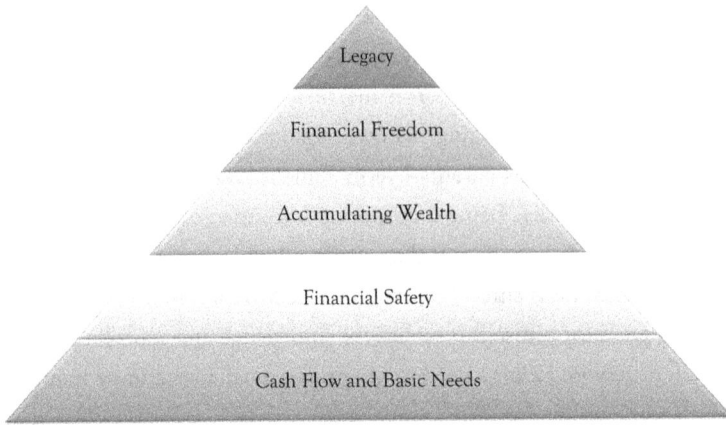

Figure 1.3 Need hierarchy for financial needs

through his protection and emergency buckets. He has the choice of spending more on his daily expenses, but coming from a middle-income family he thought it wiser to live simply with more funds for cushion. In future, if needed after his marriage, he could lower the proportion under these two heads and his income also may increase and be supplemented by his wife's income as he preferred marrying a working woman. At the next stage comes the need to invest and accumulate wealth. This is where the individual after having covered the basic and accidental expenses starts looking for "investment" options, which could give him a good rate of return and also take care of his retirement-related expenses. (While we are mentioning here as individual, this includes family or household as a unit.) There are options of paying down any debts taken, for example, house loan or vehicle loan. The focus then shifts to assets for long-term success and longevity. Since Rajesh had a good income, he could do this at his present age and thus he invested around 30 percent of his income in long-term instruments. At the next stage is the need for children education. The stages are not strictly categorized and there is an overlap often possible. Spending on vacations and any long-term asset is often done at this stage of financial freedom. Presently, Rajesh kept only 5 percent for this but he thought of moving this up to 20 percent as he could foresee the need for educating two children. Also at this stage the financial needs become linked with esteem needs, such as self-respect and personal accomplishment, and there are chances of the purchase of luxurious goods and services that uplift the status. The highest level at the stage of self-actualization as per Maslow's need hierarchy is the next stage. Estate plans, tax planning, and business succession planning all fall within this category. Rajesh did not plan for this currently although he decided to revisit his financial plan five years later. The path laid down here is a general one, whereas age, gender, household size, family stage, and occupation may bring in differences.

It may also be considered that as life expectancy has increased, people are now concerned about having sufficient savings during their retirement phase—across all income levels. Fifty percent of the lower income group Americans are anxious about their retirement savings, whereas in upper income group **26 percent** are concerned about their savings (Table 1.1).

One of the primary concerns among many Americans is debt, because of the increasing cost of education and health care. Average costs of annual college, for instance, have escalated 25 percent in the last 10 years, whereas the household debt of the United States has grown twofold (i.e., $14 trillion approximately) since 2004. While this is just an illustration, the situation is similar in other countries as well. After the satisfaction of these abovementioned needs people could shift their attention to higher orders financial needs in hierarchy, for instance, legacy-focused items, such as estate and tax planning, or business succession planning.

Table 1.1 Individual's concern about savings

Worry about each of the following often	Lower Income	Middle Income	Upper Income
Saving for retirement	50%	37%	26%
Settling their bills	59%	35%	15%
The proportion of debt they have	51%	35%	21%
The cost of family health care	47%	35%	18%
Take a compensation reduction cut due to reduced hours or demand for their work	51%	25%	18%
Loss of their jobs	40%	21%	11%

Source: Pew Research Center, survey of U.S. adults conducted April 7–12, 2020.

On the basis of one's financial need, SMART (i.e., Specific, Measurable, Achievable, Relevant, and Timely) goals should be set. Formulating a plan that keeps one's goals on priority is the best approach to achieve financial goals. In the previous section, Rajesh could divide his financial goals into short-term (a year or so), medium-term (three to five years), and long-term goals (over five years). Short-term goals may also include things like buying a mobile/laptop or paying the fees of first year of college. Medium-term goals could include owning a four-wheeler on a loan of three to four years. Long-term goals, whereas, could be possessing a home or planning for the retirement. The goal-setting process would need a person to prioritize and choose the goals that he or she desires to attain. In accordance with the plans and goal an estimate of money and time would be required. Subsequently, the resources are matched in order to achieve the goals step by step. Refer to Appendix 1 for a sample budget sheet. The budget is revisited and tailored to the goals from short term to long term.

3. Execution

At this stage, many times a financial adviser or consultant with an expert opinion is needed. He/she would develop a strategy for your financial plan. While developing the strategy, based on the financial goals, different forms of loan and investment opportunities available in the market are searched and then the best mix of options suited to the individual's need is set.

Example of Anya and Arhann's Personal Financial Plan

Suppose, Anya and Arhann who are in their early 30s would like to draw up a financial plan. They fill up a worksheet of their personal financial statement to get to know about their financial standing. They are a double income no kids (DINK) couple and for the last five years they have not prepared a concrete financial plan for the future. Nonetheless, they have invested in numerous assets of different types and in life insurance plans.

Assets Assessment

Arhann works as an investor in real estate, and Anya is an online entrepreneur. Arhann makes $120,000 a year, whereas Anya makes around $25,000.

- Assets they presently own:
- $200,000 in cash, bank accounts, and money market accounts;
- Bonds and stocks in a brokerage account: current value of $620,000, base of $300,000;
- Arhann has $720,000 in 401(k) savings, with a 6 percent job match;
- $600,000 in Anya's SEP IRA;
- Arhann is the proud owner of a $140,000 automobile. The amount owed on the car loan is $50,000. He has had his car for the past two-and-a-half years. The pair lives in a $660,000 home. They secured a $140,000 loan with a 6.5 percent interest rate.

Insurance Coverage

The couple has life insurance plans.

- Arhann has $400,000 in life insurance via his job and pays a monthly payment of at least $250;
- Anya commits to a whole life insurance with a $85,000 death benefit, a $30,000 cash value, and a $20,000 base for a monthly premium of $150.

Retirement Expenses

- If Arhann retires at the age of 45, he will get a pension equal to at least 40 percent of his highest average earnings ($140,000) for the rest of his life;

- Annuity for retirement ($350,000 current value, $230,000 basis);
- Arhann contributes the maximum amount to his 401(k) account each year;
- Anya, on the other hand, is self-employed and does not have a pension plan.

Joint Expenses

- The couple spends about $11,000 per month on supplies and living expenditures such as utilities, entertainment, food, property taxes, and other things.
- Arhann's social security benefits will be $8,050 per month when he becomes 60, and she decides to apply for it at retirement or at an eligible age. They have no will and intend to stay childless for the rest of their lives.

4. Monitoring and Reassessment

The last step of the financial planning process encompasses observing and controlling the implementation process of financial plans and its advancement toward achieving goals, as the world is ever changing. Owing to constant changes, it is wise to keep the financial plans updated. Financial planning is an active process that requires continuous observing and modification of financial plans and targets. Setting goals, gathering data, measuring progress, and changing course if required are all part of the financial planning process. Financial strategies are evaluated and updated on a regular basis.

Is a Continuing Process

The aim of having healthy finances is to ensure that plans are in control and this controlling process is effective. Through constant monitoring, it is possible to discover any issues and sort out before it ruins portfolio. It is advisable to monitor and review your plan at least once in a year. In the best-case scenario, on realization that certain aspects or details in financial plan have changed a revision in financial plan occurs. But majorly it is contingent on the financial features that one is evaluating. For instance, one should check savings account consistently, at least monthly. Nevertheless, most of the people do this more frequently as they regularly use these accounts. Thus, it is significant to monitor financial plan and modify accordingly in changing times, as elements of personal finance have an inclination to change. A slight change in these elements (budgets, investments, financial risks, estate plan, etc.) can severely affect the ability to meet financial planning and life goals. By regular monitoring, a healthy and rewarding financial plan could be devised and can prevent life altering and devastating consequences.

In sum, personal finance is an imperative part of human's life. Taking financial decisions that are wise is an important aspect of life. With right attitude and discipline in money management, one can achieve financial goals faster.

Marketing for Retail Financial Products

The American Marketing Association's (2017) definition of Marketing emphasizes it as the science or art of acquiring, maintaining and growing customers through creation, communication, and delivering of value. The definition is to be considered from an organizational function but it has the customer at heart. Thus marketing has an important functional role in organizational decision making and execution, and this holds true for companies dealing in financial products. While a detailed customer side view of financial services and the decision making involved will be discussed in Chapters 2 and 3, the company side planning and positioning of the products is explained here.

All financial service product companies have to choose along the types of products they would want to offer and the operational procedures to be followed to create them. The strategic marketing planning starts at the corporate level (Figure 1.4). Aligned to the strategic intent of an organization, institutional goals are set, key competencies identified, environment scanned for opportunities and threats, and a positioning statement is developed for each service product to be offered by the firm to specific

MARKET ANALYSIS	• Size • Composition • Location • Trends	Define, Analyze Market Segments	
		Select Target Segments to Serve	
INTERNAL ANALYSIS	• Resources • Reputation • Constraints • Values	Articulate Desired Position in Market	Marketing Action Plan
		Select Benefits to Emphasize to Customers	
COMPETITIVE ANALYSIS	• Strengths • Weaknesses • Current Positioning	Analyze Possibilities for Differentiation	

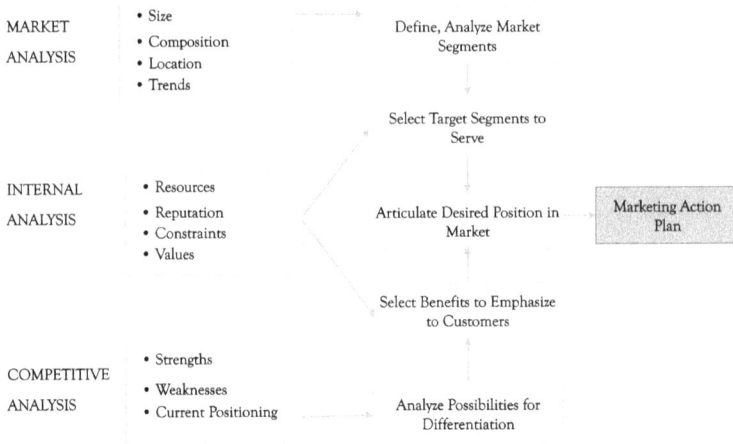

Figure 1.4 Strategic marketing plan

market segments. The positioning strategy would be developed by following the given steps:

1. Definition and analysis of market segments: While scanning the environment, the firm must define the market segments based on some of the population from the demographic, socioeconomic, geographic, behavioral, or psychographic characteristics. It is the decision of the management to see which segmentation bases would best work for their products.

2. Market targeting: After the segmentation is done, the next task for the firm is to identify the specific target markets that it wants to serve.

3. Internal corporate analysis: While deciding the target markets, the firm also has to assess its resources and match with the service offering that is to be offered. The constraints are also identified.

4. Developing the positioning statement: Based on the analysis till now and identifying the target segments, it becomes important to identify which benefit(s) needs to be emphasized and that is developed into a positioning statement, which offers answers to the following questions.

5. An example of the positioning statement is given as follows.

6. Competitive analysis: It is also important to understand the competitive marketplace and identify the competitor's strengths and weaknesses. This will have an impact on the positioning statement.
7. Finally, the key points of parity and differentiation have to be identified and the differentiation factors highlighted through all marketing communication messages.

The positioning strategy has to be aligned with the operating assets available to the firm. The firm must check if it can build or allocate the necessary physical facilities, equipment, technology, and human resource as outlined in the positioning strategy. The financial viability in the long term of the firm with the desired positioning also has to be checked.

In the next step, the firm has to develop the service marketing concept or the value proposition that would be able to clearly identify the benefits offered to customers and the costs incurred by the firm. As per the flower of service concept, the financial institution will have to identify both the core and supplementary aspects of the service product offering. The reliability levels of these services have to be established as per the customer preference and firm's reach. An understanding of how, where, and when would the customer access the services is also important to be looked at. This would ask for an understanding of customer resources that is, time, money, and effort that would include mental as well as physical effort.

The service operations concept also has to be defined at this stage, which would help in understanding the geographic spread, requisite scheduling of operations, and facilities layout and design. It would clarify the role of intermediaries and customers as well as the design of the front stage and backstage activities.

Together, the two concepts of service marketing and service operation in the organization influence the design of the service delivery. The customer is always offered a bundle of core product along with a variety of supplementary services. As products, markets, and customers of the BFSI sector mature, the supplementary services start offering differentiation through these value-added supplementary services. The relationships and emotional connect between the organization's employee and customer also becomes important.

Flower of Service Concept

The flower of service concept as laid down by Lovelock (1996) is a classification framework that can help the financial services organizations to identify and classify different supplementary services that are wanted by the customers. All potential supplementary services can be classified into the eight clusters as shown in Figure 1.5.

The abovementioned eight clusters can be grouped in two broad categories based on whether they are facilitating the service delivery process or are enhancing the core product value.

Information: Customers frequently need information regarding several terms and conditions of the financial product. It is important for a financial organization to make this information accessible through different means.

Order taking: Customers need to be provided with the knowledge of what is available and what is not and may need assurance regarding delivery. The process needs to be swift and smooth.

Billing: Customers should have the knowledge of how much they have to pay. All the details regarding payments ought to be accurate, clear, and lucid.

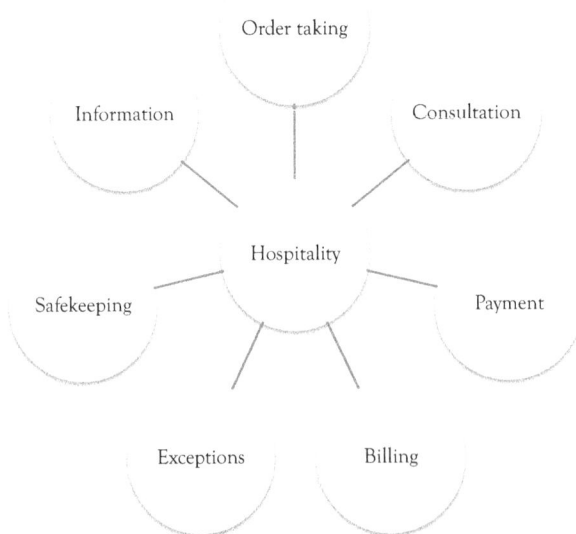

Order taking

Consultation

Information

Hospitality

Safekeeping

Payment

Exceptions

Billing

Figure 1.5 The flower of service

Payment: Customers can pay happily and swiftly, provided the transaction processes are easy, user-friendly, and convenient to use.

Consultation: Value addition to the financial products can be facilitated through providing customized advice and consultation based on customer's requirement and circumstances. This is of particular importance in financial products and may serve as a basis for differentiation against competitors.

Hospitality: Customers deserve to be considered as guests when they visit a business and use its services as they invest their time and effort in it. Thus, the facility design and layout have to be designed accordingly.

Safekeeping: Customers do not like to tense over caring about the personal belongings that they have with them. They must sense safety in their transactions whether physical or electronic. This aspect has to be provided for, in the design of operations.

Exceptions: When customers make special requests they appreciate some flexibility and when things do not go as per plan they expect responsiveness. The employees and procedures at a financial institution must be trained to deal with that.

Thus, it can be realized that for financial service products, apart from the core product there are several facilitating and enhancing supplementary services that can be looked as a competitive advantage. Organizations dealing in retail financial products, whether banks, insurance companies, NBFCs or any other firm, need to develop these competencies based on their organizational strengths because as competition increases the customers become more knowledgeable and demanding. These services help in catering to their demand. Therefore the role of people, processes including technology and physical evidence (tangible cues) comes upfront and needs to be well integrated into the marketing strategy. The marketing mix for the financial products companies hence comprises of 7Ps and not 4Ps. To be exact, the 7Ps are people, price, product, place, physical evidence, processes, and promotion.

Conclusion

This chapter presents the need to understand the financial products planning from a customer perspective by financial organizations while introducing different types of financial products and different needs of customers. The chapter establishes the need for having a sound marketing strategy for the financial organizations. The key takeaways from this chapter are:

i. A comprehensive understanding of financial products.
ii. The individual financial planning process.
iii. The need for marketing strategy for a financial products company.
iv. A framework for identifying the characteristic features of financial products.

CHAPTER 2

Distinctive Features of Retail Financial Products as Services and Consumer Decision Making

Chapter Overview

This chapter starts by providing distinctive features of financial service products and their classification on different criteria that would help financial organizations in rolling out their marketing strategy. The chapter then talks about the consumer decision-making process and the critical points that need to be taken care of by the financial organizations. It introduces the concepts of service encounter, service script, and service blueprint to manage satisfactory firm customer interaction for a financial company. The role of culture and how to deal with misbehaving customers has also been dealt with in detail in this chapter. The author introduces a framework for customer satisfaction in the purchase journey in this chapter, which is based out of field research.

Characteristics of Financial Products as Services

Classification schemes in marketing help marketing theorists and practitioners by offering important insights but with its set of limitations. Many financial services organizations are dominated by an operations orientation. But marketing concepts bring a cross-disciplinary orientation leading to generation of more number of effective strategies. There are several service classification schemes based on characteristics of financial service products that can offer managerial value. They can be categorized on the nature of service activity, manner of service delivery, nature of demand, attributes of service experience, customer relationships, and level of customization. Before moving to the classification schemes based on different kind of categorizations, it would be relevant to discuss the basic characteristics of financial services that have marketing implications. Financial services may be considered different from the tangible goods in four aspects: intangibility, variability, simultaneity, and perishability. A detailed explanation of these with reference to the retail financial services is given in the following sections.

Intangibility

Financial services are intangible, that is, one cannot feel or touch them directly. They can only be experienced and need to be seen as processes and activities. Thus these products cannot be stored and though largely consistent by nature, in case of demand fluctuations they become difficult to manage. Quality is difficult to assess and pricing is also difficult as determining a unit of service is not easy. Challenges are involved in deciding on the information to be placed in their promotional messages. These products contain legal and financial expertise and are crafted with a lot of terms and conditions. The transition to services from goods may be seen as a continuum between tangibility and intangibility. The goods that are high of the tangibility dominant are easy to be evaluated on their features by prospects and customers, whereas the products that are high on the intangibility side are difficult to evaluate. This feature has implications on the consumer decision making.

The term "search qualities" was coined by Nelson (1974) to define those brand qualities that "the consumer can determine by inspection prior to purchase" and "experience qualities" to refer to those that "are not determined prior to purchase." Darby and Karni (1973) added that some qualities can never be confirmed by an average consumer. This occurs due to lack of sufficient technical expertise of a consumer to evaluate the product's actual performance, to identify his/her own need for the product or service, or as spotting a need discretely from filling the need at the same time is uneconomical or difficult. These qualities have been labeled as "credence." The financial services lie on the extreme of intangibility and thus require high level of credence-related attributes to help customer in the decision-making process. These products need greater involvement of the customer, are high in risk, and demand intensity and focus in terms of time and effort.

To deal with the intangibility dimension, firms must take care of the following in their marketing strategies:

- Offer tangible proof
  - Symbolic cues (i.e., uniforms, logos);
  - Tangible cues (i.e., membership cards, ticket, certificates).
- Lessen risk
  - Highlight reputation and qualifications;
  - Service assurances;
  - Notify and teach customers.

Heterogeneity

Financial services may be seen as performances involving human beings and hence they would not be exactly alike in different instances whether it is with reference to the customers or the employees. Ensuring service quality is thus a challenge and control of several factors contributing to quality is not possible, such as the ability of an individual to clearly articulate the financial needs, the knowledge and skill of the employee to meet those needs, and the role of other customers and employees while a service transaction is taking place. A service encounter is defined as the interaction between the service employee/equipment and the customer. Service quality fluctuates across service encounters and results in creating moments of truth (positive or negative) for the customer. Service people are crucial to service delivery. The strategies that financial companies can use for managing variability are:

- Customer surveys and feedback;
- Training in interpersonal and technical skills;
- Offer product knowledge;
- Make sure backstage systems support frontline staff;

- Employ standardization strategies
- franchising, scripts;
- Insert quality into all processes.

Simultaneous Production and Consumption

- As services are intangibles, they are not similar to goods that are produced prior to consumption or sell, instead services are produced and consumed concurrently. For example, when an insurance agent explains different terms and conditions of several insurance policies (products) the customer has to consume that information to process for taking any decision. It is worth mentioning that employees are a part of deliverables or a package and are of significance in customer's service experience. Thus, from marketing implications perspective there is no mass production possible. The one-to-one service transaction happens in real time and customer satisfaction is dependent on that. Unless until the individual is convinced about a financial product, he would not proceed toward purchase and this has to be done by the processes, point of interactions, and design of the products and employees. The strategies for managing inseparability in financial services organization are:
- Manage the service encounter:
    - Employee scripts and roles
    - Front-line staff need both technical and interpersonal skills (recruit and train)
    - Educate the customer (provider–marketer)
- Manage customer interactions;
- Manage the physical evidence;
- Develop customer service policies and service recovery procedures.

Perishability

Financial services cannot be kept for future use or reuse, or be given back in a physical sense. They can only be kept in memories. Thus, demand management principles for this start differing from physical goods and so do the concepts related to customer satisfaction. The strategies to manage supply and demand are:

- Using creative pricing techniques;
- Including reservation/queuing systems;
- Cross train employees;
- Flexibly use the fixed space.

Framework for Classifying and Analyzing Customer Financial Products

The retail financial products are essentially service products that require heavy customer involvement in terms of customer's time, effort, and money. It is also to be understood that this product requires a very high level of credibility as money is a possession, which is always a scarce and precious resource for an individual. Talking about the financial products as services it has to borne in mind that these are a continuous series of "deeds, acts or performances." The first classification scheme that we discuss for managerial decision making revolves around the "inseparability" characteristic along with the above two facts. There are two important questions to be answered by managers here, "at whom is the service activity directed" and "is the activity tangible or intangible" as shown in Figure 2.1. In case of financial service products, the service activity is intangible and directed at possessions, that is money, and can be classified within the category of "Information Processing Services." These kinds of services have been revolutionized by ICT technologies. However, these require technically qualified professional manpower along with the Internet and machines to deliver. Information is in intangible form and can be transformed into tangibles as a report, document, or a presentation, and so on, and could be delivered by people. While the physical presence is not mandatory for the customer to interact with the place of service delivery, firms have to decide as to what points of contacts can be generated for the same. Habit and traditions may also have a role to play in the means of contact between the customer and the firm.

	Who or What Is the Direct Recipient of the Service?	
Nature of the Service Act	People	Possessions
Tangible Actions	People processing (Services directed at people's bodies): • Barbers • Health care	Possessions processing (Services directed at physical possessions): • Refueling
Intangible Actions	Mental stimulus processing (Services directed at people's mind): • Education • Advertising/PR	Information processing (Services directed at intangible services): • Accounting • Banking

Figure 2.1 Classification of services

The implications of this categorization for financial services as information processing services offers the following insights:

- **Designing the service benefits**: Marketing managers for financial products need to aptly recognize the key benefits, which a customer may be looking for and accordingly design the service process. For example, consumers want lesser processing time for the housing loans. Knowing this fact, the lending financial organizations need to accordingly put up a process in place and also train its employees appropriately so that the processing time for house loans remains minimum.
- **Delivering customer experiences**: It is known that a satisfied customer is a priced possession. To deliver customer satisfaction, financial organizations need to take care of the various service encounters that the customer may have with different touch points, exterior and interior appearance and features of service facilities, the characteristics and behavior of the target audience to drive a satisfactory or delightful customer experience.

Based on how and where the service needs to be delivered can be the basis for the next classification scheme. Retail financial lending organizations are today operating at multiple sites and at times the service employees also visit the customer houses and offices for service delivery purposes. The customer visiting the branches is rare. Apart from face-to-face interactions, the information technology today has enabled web-based service interactions and delivery for the financial products' customers.

Retail financial organizations are subject to the market conditions that fluctuate heavily, be it the subprime mortgage crisis in 2008 or the Brexit in 2016, it impacted the financial conditions of all economies. The demand in retail financial products is also subjected to the changes in the domestic and global economy and accordingly has an implication on the marketing strategy to raise or meet the demand.

When we talk of retail financial services, the attribute of service delivery would use an almost equal combination of service equipment and people. Thus, while evaluating different competing options while taking purchase decision, customers may establish criteria that are based on this combination rather than the service output. Retail financial institutions need to identify the extent to which these attributes would play a role in customer decision making. They can then also look at within industry bench marks on these as well as insights from other industries can be used to design the service delivery experience. In financial products, since money is involved, people look for tangible cues that can signal credibility. It is for this reason that while equipment may ease delivery processes, human beings lend physical shape to the product. Additionally, the duration of benefits and the duration of service benefits could also be looked at by retail financial organizations when designing the service delivery.

A very important classification scheme can be based on the type of relationship that a retail financial organization aims to have with its customers; should it be a formal relationship like memberships or no formal relationship and should it be of a continuous or discrete nature. Retail financial organizations can implement a membership-based continuous service relationship because the product is itself continuous in nature. Thus banks, insurance companies, NBFCs, and so on must not adopt a transaction-based orientation in marketing. It is already known that retaining customers is much more profitable than acquiring customers.

With a continuous focus the organizations have more knowledge about their customers, which can be used for the purposes of segmentation, targeting specific marketing communications and pricing. The customer loyalty would increase and so would the possibility of increasing the purchase basket both in volume and price. The room for customization would also be more.

Consumer Decision Making

The consumer decision-making process can be classified into three stages: prepurchase, purchase, and postpurchase, based on the basic model. The prepurchase phase comprises the information search and assessment of alternatives.

Information search: The prospective customer for a financial product uses several sources for information search that comprise individual sources such as friends, relatives, and other reference groups. There are a host of nonpersonal sources also available these days such as mass or selective media. In digital age consumers get the required information at the click of the mouse. However, given the nature of financial products, customers tend to rely more on personal sources. Traditional and digital mass media earlier provided information about search-related attributes more than personal experiences but now the latter has also increased. So both electronic and physical word of mouth become important to build credibility.

In services the personal information becomes central as the complexity of product increases and the objective standards to assess the product decreases. This happens in the financial products. Consumers also look for postpurchase information more than in any other products as many times certain attributes of the product can only be learnt through experience. They cannot be learnt before purchase.

The **perceived risk** component in financial products is higher than in any other product for several reasons such as intangibility, implication of the decisions take longer time in outcomes, nonstandardized product and lesser search qualities before the purchase. There is a component of uncertainty always attached to financial products because they cannot be consumed immediately, and money, by its nature, is precious and people want to be safe with that; also, the time value of money is an important moderator in the purchase decision. Unlike goods financial products do not have guarantees or warranties attached, these can only be communicated by people, the brand equity, design of operations, and putting suitable terms and conditions in place. The experiences of financial products cannot be returned and service recovery becomes another dimension that financial organizations need to take care of. The lack of knowledge of a particular financial product also makes it difficult to evaluate his response and satisfaction to it. Thus, the perceived risk component is very high for financial products and demand consumer-friendly strategies to deal with it.

Evaluation of Alternatives

The evoked set: Given the personal conditions of an individual, the consumer would generate an evoked set that would comprise of products that a consumer is willing to consider in his purchase decision. Since the evoked set of financial products would be smaller than any consumer good, there are chances that a customer would pick up the first acceptable alternative on the basis of his experience or interaction with it. This could be on the basis of a personal interaction, a digital interaction or an interaction with equipment such as ATM. Sometimes it may be a combination of three.

It is important to note that customer satisfaction, which is normally studied as a postpurchase construct, is important as a consequent at every stage. Figure 2.2 illustrates the consumer decision-making stages across prepurchase, purchase, and postpurchase stage with the key marketing decision issues and the service providers touch points highlighted.

Factors to Be Considered While Designing Customer Interactions During Financial Service Product Purchase and Consumption

Emotions and moods: Emotions and moods are affective states that affect customer's perceptions and experiential evaluation that they may have had. Moods are different from emotions as they are transient states, which may happen at a specific time and in a specific situation. Emotions on the other hand are more intense, pervasive, and stable.

SERVICE QUALITY (SURVEY)

Customer Stages	Key Concepts	Service Provider
Awareness of Need	Need Arousal	Company/Other sources (Aggregators, personal)
Information Search • Clarify Needs • Explore Solutions • Identify alternate solutions and providers	Evoked Set	Company Other Sources (Aggregators, personal)
Evaluation of Alternatives • Review Supplier and Third Party Information • Discussion with Service Personnel • Get Advice and Feedback	Credence Attributes Perceived Risk Formation of Expectation around Product and Service	Company Other Sources (Aggregators, personal)

PREPURCHASE STAGE

SERVICE QUALITY

Customer Stages	Key Concepts	Service Provider
Request Service from Chosen Supplier Payment and Formalities Service Delivery by Personnel	Moments of Truth Service Encounter Role and Script Theories	Company and Third Party

PURCHASE STAGE

Satisfaction

Customer Stages	Key Concepts	Service Provider
Evaluation of Service Performance Future Intentions	Confirmation/Disconfirmation of Expectations Satisfaction Delight Repurchase Word-of-Mouth	Service Personnel
SERVICE QUALITY		

POSTPURCHASE STAGE

Satisfaction

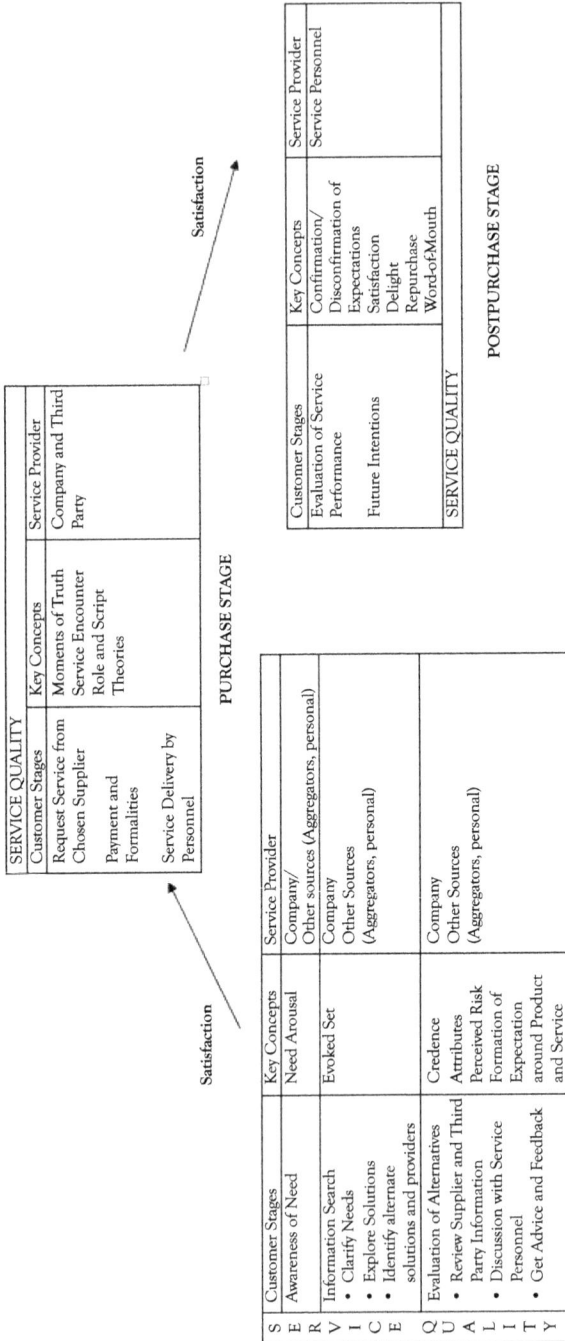

Figure 2.2 Consumer decision making

Since the experiential qualities are high in financial products, affective states like emotions and moods have a significant part in influencing the perception of effectiveness of a service interaction/encounter. A service interaction or encounter occurs when a consumer comes in straight contact of a service provider that may include a one-to-one interaction and an in-person experience. When a customer has an encounter with a service in a sullen and angry mood, the chances of his interpreting the service experience negatively increase. Similarly, if in a service facility, the encounter between a customer and the service provider turns out negative, chances are that the other customer's mood also will get negative and the perception of effective service may have negative implications. Thus, since services involve people as a part of experience managing customer emotions and mood become important for the financial products organizations. A customer in a positive mood would follow instructions given by these organizations better and also judge service encounters better. Emotions and moods improve and extend the experiences making them either more positive or negative. Moods and emotions also have an impact in the manner the information about the service provider is received, absorbed, transferred, and retrieved.

Postpurchase Evaluation

Customers of financial products may attribute the reasons for their dissatisfaction to the financial organization, any intermediary or staff involved, or themselves. Customers play an important role in defining their needs and availing customized financial solutions; thus, many times they feel responsible in case of dissatisfaction. It becomes important thus to help the customer identify his role in the service delivery system. In case of satisfied customers, financial firms must strive toward achieving loyalty. Brand loyalty may also happen because of high costs, efforts, and difficulty in switching the brands. The financial organization, however, needs to be sure and certain about their own product and supplementary services apart from these reasons for customer to stay.

Using Drama as a Metaphor for Designing Financial Product Experience

Scholarly marketing research and practice in service business have often compared the provision of services akin to drama as they both try to form and hold a favorable impression in front of the audiences (Grove and Fisk 1992). Also, it has been recognized that this kind of outcome can be achieved by managing the physical settings and actors' behavior. A service marketer actually plays many drama-related roles such as writer, director, and choreographer to ensure that the audiences (customers) are pleased with the performance they experience. This holds true for all retail financial organizations. In terms of designing the operations and training employees, financial organization marketers realize how the skill of their employees (service actors) in performing their roles, their appearance, and their commitment to every performance is central to the service delivery. The service encounters where human actors are more in contact are more specifically related to this concept and also in cases where the service employees have room for using discretion.

The physical setting of a service encounter among a financial business and the customer is to be thought of like a stage where the drama is to be enacted. The scenery, props, and physical cues all combine together with the actors to achieve a desired performance. The distinctive features of a physical setting include: color and brightness, pitch and volume of sounds, temperature of the air, freshness, smells, movements, the comfort and style of the furnishings, the design of the setting, cleanliness, and use of space. Many times these settings become a source of the competitive advantage for financial organizations. The drama metaphor has proved a very effective manner of conceptualizing the service encounters. The aspects that can be considered similar and processes be activated are: selection of employees (audition), training (rehearsal), designing the service environment (setting of the stage), defining the roles (writing performance scripts), and deciding the activities to be performed in front of the customer (on stage) and back end (back stage).

Coming to designing service roles and scripts, it is important to first define what roles are. Roles could be defined as a group of social cues that affect and regulate behavior in a particular setting (Zeithaml and Bitner 2000). A well-set role for both employees and customers and their acting out the role are determinants for the success of a service performance at the financial institution. It is also significant to comprehend the interaction's nature as it will have an implication of the role in general and the one in a specific situation.

In general, there are three types of customer and employee roles: autonomy, dependence, and cooperation. Considering financial products, customers have now adapted a dominant role rather than dependent on the employees in some situations due to increased exposure and knowledge sharing.

It is also necessary that employees in the service industry do their job as per the customer expectations, or else the customers would be dissatisfied or frustrated. Similarly, customers also have to play their role well. Educated and informed customers who know what is to be done in the service interaction and who also cooperate with the employees are going to get the best results of a service encounter.

Designing Service Scripts

Subsequent to knowing the analogy between services and drama, an imperative factor that impacts service performance positively is script designing. A script is a series of logical events anticipated by a person involving himself/herself either as an observer or as a member (Zeithaml and Bitner 2000). In sum, a service script comprises a battery of systematic actions, performers, and stuffs that ensemble together to demonstrate the expectations of customers (Zeithaml and Bitner 2000). Meeting the requirements of a service script would lead to customer satisfaction and deviation would lead to customer frustration. Thus, service system designers and service employees at a bank must give attention to the service scripts. Appendix 2 shows examples of several customer interaction scripts over a call for a bank. It is also important to note by financial product marketers that deviations from a customer's expected script whether positive or negative may detract them or add to their experience.

The Other Customers

In high-contact service encounters in any financial institution there are other customers also present on the stage. They play a very important role of giving company to each other, but if it starts overcrowding then there would be dissatisfaction among customers because of the harassment caused. Similarly the behavior of other customers also influences the satisfaction or dissatisfaction of all the customers. Differences in demographics, psychographics, and personality traits can result in incompatible customer behaviors. Marketers for financial products need to manage with tact the presence of these customers in the same service setting.

What Is Customer Misbehavior?

There are some distinct sets of customer misbehavior in every company; however, there are a few issues that are constant in every industry. Mentioned below are some of the tips on how to find and resolve them.

When customers go against the accepted norm of a business and harms or interrupts its activities in some way or other, it is known as customer misbehavior or consumer misbehavior.

For instance, breaking a window/door, bullying an employee or doing a physical harm, and so on, comes under customer behavior. Not only these serious ones but simpler ones like disregarding the rules of a business premise/workplace also involve misbehavior. The term, "**JAYCustomers**," was coined in 1994 by Christopher Lovelock; like "jaywalkers" to denote common misbehaviors by customers:

1. The thief: These are the ones who shoplift, get into movies without tickets, pay through stolen debit and credit cards, and so on. Their ultimate goal is to avoid payment for products and services.
2. The rulebreaker: These are the ones who pay no regard to warning signs in a premise and/or requests from the employees of a business and often found in spaces inside the premise or using things they are not supposed to.
3. The belligerent: These are the ones who are often in a huff or are intoxicated and are willing to involve in an argument or fight, which

may also include physical and verbal abuse of the employees of a business.

4. The cheat: These are the ones who are similar to the rulebreakers but are more clever. They know how to avail themselves of the opportunity by manipulation and fraud and believes in "100 per cent satisfaction guarantee" philosophy but to their advantage and in order to exploit.

5. The family feuder: These are the ones who involve in scuffles or arguments with their own family or with their friends and can pull nearby customers and employees as well into the arguments/fights.

6. The vandal: These are the ones who cause harm to a business property by breaking, burning, tearing, and other destructive activities.

What Are the Reasons Behind Customer's Misbehavior?

There are many reasons. For instances:

- Some customers do it due to poverty, whereas some do just to get a thrill or a feeling of excitement.
- The motives behind vandalism could be fun or to protest or to show resentment toward a business or maybe just out of behavior.
- Some customers could be belligerent as they think that by being rude or intimidating they can strike a good deal or they just want to enhance their own sense of worthiness and often perceive sales people as easy targets.
- In some cases, some customers do it out of their role and power consciousness. When a business fails to meet their expectations, they want to leverage their position as a customer by showing their anger or by intimidating/abusing employees of that business.

The Effects of Customer Misbehavior

The behaviors of jaycustomers often jeopardize the brand, affects its employees, and the customers who are not jaycustomers.

Behaviors of jaycustomers cause issues to the employees, such as:

- Increased burnout;
- Tendency to be rude with customers;
- Job disinterest.

Jaycustomers affect the perception of normal customers about the service quality and business as a whole. For example, if a family feuder is behaving badly and having arguments with his/her family members or friends and the staff is acting as a mute spectator or are frightened to stop it or handling it in an improper way, the next time, the normal customer would think twice before coming to that place again.

Finally, jaycustomers have a negative effect on the overall business.

When customers steal/shoplift, vandalize the property, and cheat and manipulate for their benefits cumulatively affects the bottom line. It damages the brand reputation and increases emotional labor among employees.

How to Tackle Bad Behaviors of Jaycustomers?

When incidents of misbehaviors from jaycustomers arise in a business premise, often employees find and learn to deal with such situations at least emotionally. These emotional ways of dealing often manifest in different forms like ignoring or showing indifference to jaycustomers, venting out bottled up feelings toward each other, giving emotional support to each other, and so on. Even if these temporary coping tactics help, it does not solve the problem in the long run. For dealing with such problems in the long run, management must intervene and should deploy the following six generic strategies in order to minimize the occurrence and to alleviate the effects of misbehavior.

1. Selective Recruitment

When it comes to handling jaycustomers and their behaviors, some people are better than others. A manager should look out for such employees, specifically who have good social skills, greater self-confidence, and who do not agitate easily. They can be good frontline employees in cases of jaycustomers.

These "anti-jaycustomer" employees can maintain their cool during a tussle and could pacify an agitated and fuming customer. Tackling jaycustomers can exhaust even an empathetic and articulate employee in the long run, so having someone who is thick-skinned would fit well to handle such belligerent and fraud customers.

2. Changes to Training and Induction Procedures

Even though incidences of misconduct by customers happen quite frequently, a lot of organizations, often small ones, fail to include trainings in their formal induction process to deal with jaycustomers. For instance, a group of call center employees are exposed to verbal aggression at least 10 times per day.

Organizations that introduced training regarding misconducts comprised techniques like role-playing, recordings, or a standard operating procedures kind of information to deal with jaycustomers. Such steady and simple efforts toward misbehavior contribute to the emotional well-being of employees.

3. Enhanced Rewards

Employees who are subjected to jaycustomers and their bad behaviors experience greater stress. Hence, rewarding them by praise, extra pay, flexible shifts, promotions, and so on could be done.

These add-ons to employees help them to get rid of the unpleasantness attached to the job to some extent. It might not decrease the frequency of misbehavior; however, it will assist in gaining participation toward frontline positions.

In combination with selective recruitment, it is a potent way to discover and keep employees who are better at tackling misbehaving jaycustomers.

4. Team Make-Up and Design

As previously mentioned in selective recruitment, some people are better in handling jaycustomers, the same is true for teams.

These teams can be of different types, often, contingent on the type of organization and an organization's stance toward misbehavior.

Some team may contain senior employees, some may have freshers, some may contain more females or more males, and so on.

An effective and a common practice is to employ a mother figure like lady at return counters. These motherly figures are empathetic, tactful, and articulate, and people rather shy away from abusing and cheating these persons.

5. Increased Counseling

When employees encounter unpleasant experiences by jaycustomers, they tend to devise methods of counseling themselves informally by providing emotional support and venting out to each other, and so on.

These informal techniques can be formalized. For instance, by keeping an open door policy, by allowing those to voice their concerns, by keeping a timeslot for talking with an empathetic manager could assist in employee retention and boosting up morale.

Employees who are not experienced or are in a stress prone area can find this method effective, in particular.

6. Alterations to the Servicescape

Finally, businesses can modify or customize the physical aspects of a store/place to safeguard employees and suppress misconduct.

Big counters, surveillance equipment like CCTV, strong barricades, and sometimes modifications in uniform are employed to reduce the severity and occurrence of misbehavior. Nonetheless, it has been found by research that with such alterations, severity minimizes and not the rate of occurrence. Thus, it is not sensible to rely totally on it.

Customer misbehaviors could jeopardize business reputation, reduce employee morale and productivity, and hinders growth, if left unattended. Planning is the way to manage customer misbehavior. Formal trainings, selective recruitments, counseling, and customizing servicescape could be introduced to alleviate and control customer misbehavior. Lack of such structures and strategies would not keep jaycustomers away and would continually affect business and hinder the growth.

The Role of Culture

For Multinational Corporation (MNC) financial institutions, culture is an important determinant of people's behavior. It would include the way people interact with each other. Given the importance of people in financial products marketing, culture can play a role in customer satisfaction or dissatisfaction and is thus important for the marketer to incorporate this dimension into its operational concept. Culture is an important driver of human behavior both at national and international levels. It would broadly consist of the elements such as verbal and nonverbal language, customs and manners, values and attitudes, aesthetics, material culture, and education and social institutions. Culture is handed down from older generation to newer generation and can be learned and shared.

According to service encounter research (Czepiel et al. 1985; Shostock 1985; Surprenant and Solomon 1987), the service encounter is crucial in determining customer satisfaction, especially when the service is characterized by a high level of person-to-person connection (Stauss and Mang 1999). In many service circumstances, customers' freedom to choose which person would deal with them during the service interaction may be limited. As a result, clients who purchase a service may have little choice but to contact with an employee whose culture differs from their own. In these situations, the usage of "service scripts" (Stewart and Jackson 2003) is critical to fulfilling a service organization's goal of customer pleasure. According to service script literature (cf. Stewart and Jackson 2003), a screenplay will almost always necessitate exchanges between numerous actors playing different roles. The focus of this research, however, is on service encounters at the dyadic level (i.e., interaction or exchanges between a single customer and a single service employee). It has been suggested that service scripts are especially important at this level, because the service employee is the consumer's service (Surprenant and Solomon 1987), customer satisfaction with the service encounter (and thus with the service organization) is likely to be determined by how well the script is delivered. Prior research (Fitzsimmons and Fitzsimmons 2003; Jones et al. 1998; Mattila 1999) further suggests that at the dyadic level of interaction, a service script will be more effective if the customer and the employee providing the service share the same or similar culture. The issue of concern is that if they do not share the same or similar culture, factors (e.g., biases, language, etc.) associated with cultural differences are likely to have effects on the script used to facilitate the service encounter. These effects in turn, will likely have an impact on customer satisfaction with the service encounter. The financial services are a specific kind of service encounter.

Through a conceptual model, Hopkins et al. (2009) show the effects of culture on customer satisfaction with service interactions that take place within the setting of service companies. According to the authors, there is a direct link between the effectiveness of a service script and client satisfaction with a service encounter. The authors define culture as a segment of a larger society (i.e., the global society) whose members are perceived as different in some combination of the following traits by others in the society: ancestral homeland, language, religion, or race, and whose members perceive themselves as culturally distinct within the larger society. Traditionally, cultural differences between groups of people have been determined primarily by easily discernible characteristics of the individuals who make up the groupings. Physical appearance, for example, is an observable reflection of cultural differences (e.g., skin color, eye color and shape, hair texture and color, stature, body form, etc.) (cf. Alley and Schutheis 2001; Boli and Elliott 2008; Ferguson, Rhodes, and Lee 2001; Ferraro and Cummings 2007; Levin 2000; Sporer 2001). The physical look of a consumer from tribal Africa and a service personnel from India, for example, is an obvious indicator of cultural differences.

A general premise put forth by Milliken and Martins (1996) is that culture differences (especially observable variations) play a crucial impact in determining a customer's opinion of service script effectiveness during a service contact. That is, the customer's physical appearance may serve as a visual clue that she or he shares the same or comparable cultural values as the service personnel. In such instances, culture is likely to be a nonfactor, and other factors (such as personality) may influence consumer perceptions of the success of service scripts. Physical appearance, on the other hand, may serve as a visual cue to the customer that she/he does not share the same culture as the service employee, and that additional cultural differences (e.g., language) are likely to exist between them; differences that may cause the customer's experience with the service encounter (facilitated by the service script) to fall outside of his/her zone of acceptance. Language proficiency, for example, is frequently assumed to be a sign of competence (Fernandez et al. 2004), which has consequences for the success of service scripts from a communications standpoint. When there are cultural differences, the customer's language is unlikely to be the same as the service employee's native language. According to Ahmad Abuarqoub (2019), contact between people who speak different native languages increases the possibilities of unsuccessful communication. Furthermore, as Beamer (1992) points out, linguistic ability does not always imply communicative skill, even if the service employee is fluent in the customer's native tongue. For example, if the service person doesn't comprehend the intricacies of the customer's original language, he or she would most likely speak it with an accent, which is a barrier to effective intercultural communication (Chaney and Martin 2000).

In addition to demonstrating language/communication competency, the service personnel must also act in accordance with the customer's expectations for nonverbal components of the service script. In other words, it's not just what's said during the delivery of the script that matters, but also how it's said. For example, cultural differences in kinesics (e.g., body language), oculesics (e.g., eye use, symbolizing the extent to which the service employee is paying attention), proxemics (e.g., how the service employee structures the space around him or her), and paralanguage (e.g., voice volume, speed of talking, amount of silence, avoidance of silence) may impact script effectiveness (Dahl 1998). Thus it is proper:

- The bigger the perceived or genuine cultural differences between the customer and the service employee, the greater the influence these differences will have on the success of the service script.
- When the perceived or real cultural differences between the consumer and the service employee are modest, the service script will be more effective.
- When there are significant perceived or genuine cultural differences between the consumer and the service employee, the service script will be less effective.

The concept of cultural identification strength refers to how much a client identifies with his or her own culture. This definition is based on social identity theory (Tajfel and Turner 1979), which emphasizes inter-group interactions. Identification is one aspect of social identity theory. The operational description of this component is that the client identifies with a particular cultural group and believes that the service employee identifies with a different cultural group due to observed cultural dispar-ities. Categorization is another aspect of social identity theory. The ten-dency for a customer (who identifies with a particular cultural group) to categorize a service employee (who the customer perceives as identifying with a different cultural group) into a self-defined category with charac-teristics that may elicit positive or negative affective behaviors from the customer is known as categorizing. According to Milliken and Martins (1996), categorizing people based on observable distinctions (identifica-tion) is likely to elicit responses that are based on biases, prejudices, or preconceptions. Other studies (e.g., Akerlof and Kranton 2005; Fisher et al. 2008; Hogg and Terry 2000; Hopkins and Hopkins 2002; Sulman et al. 2007) suggests that the form of such responses is determined by the degree to which individuals identify with their respective culture. To put it another way, according to studies on self-categorization theory (Turner et al. 1987), if culture is not important to an individual's self-worth or distinctiveness (weak cultural identification), the answers are not always negative. The primary takeaway here is that visible cultural variations are identification indicators that might induce categorization actions in customers, which can provoke positive or negative responses. We may expect such answers to be greater (and based on biases, prej-udices, or preconceptions) if the customer strongly identifies with his or her culture than if the consumer does not identify strongly with his or her culture. The underlying message is that if a customer does not strongly identify with his or her culture, cultural differences (e.g., physi-cal appearance, language, demeanor) that shape a customer's perceptions of service script effectiveness are likely to be less of a factor or nonfactor during a service encounter. Based on this logic, it is logical to assume that the size of cultural variations' influence on service script efficacy is proportional to the level at which the client identifies with his or her culture. Therefore:

- The cultural identity strength moderates the effects of cultural differences on service script effectiveness.
- When the customer does not identify strongly with her/his culture, the effects of cultural differences on service script effectiveness will be less than when the customer identifies strongly with her/his culture.

The Financial Product as a Service Marketing System

A financial organization dealing with individual customers may be visualized as a system comprising of operations, delivery, and marketing elements. Parts of this system may be visible (front office/front stage) and part may not be visible (back end/backstage). The visible part could comprise of components that may relate to actors (people) or to the stage (physical setting). Customers are not interested in the backstage operations that actually are the technical core in terms of conceptualization and design of the product. The evaluation of the product is done by the service experience that the customer gets by the service interaction and experience. In addition to service operations and delivery, other components also add to the overall service evaluation by a customer. Other components comprise the sales and advertising efforts, letters, and calls from service employees. News items, bills issued by accounts departments, and other word-of-mouth communications. All of this together forms the service marketing system for the financial institution (Figure 2.3).

Blueprinting

To develop new products or modify existing ones the financial products because of the intangibility dimension are difficult to describe and depict. To live up to customer expectations on service delivery standards it becomes important to depict the service process characteristics and

			Other customers contacts
←——— Service Delivery System ———→			Advertisements in the local paper
←——— Service Operations Systems ———→			
Backstage Activities	Interior & Exterior Facilities	Other customers E.g., Friends, purchase companions	Word-of-Mouth
			Promotional Material
			Specialist Magazines
	Equipment	The Customer	P.R.Activities
			Yellow Pages
			Exhibitions
			Telephone Bookings
	Contact Personnel	Other customers E.g., Fellow customers unknown prior to the appointment	Seminars

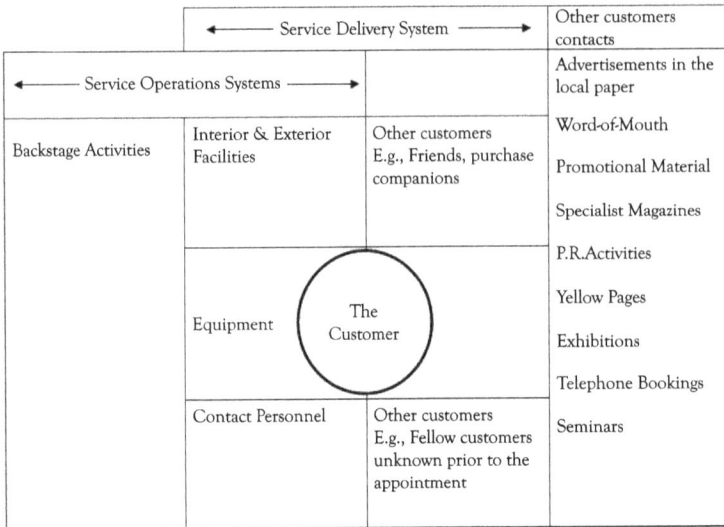

Figure 2.3 **The services marketing system**

Source: Baron and Harris 2003, p. 41.

flow to the employees, managers, and customers objectively so that they are aware about their role in it and understand the steps involved in the process. Blueprinting is a tool to help in designing the service process. A service blueprint is akin to the blueprint of manufacturing processes. It visually displays with specifications the customer touch points, visible elements involved, and the role of people. Figure 2.4 depicts a blue print for bank.

The key components of a service blue print for any financial institution would include: defining criteria for forefront events, specifying the physical proofs, identifying the major customer activities, defining communication line (customers and frontline employees), laying down the frontline activities by customer-contact employee, outlining the visibility (between front- and backstage), identifying the backstage activities by frontline employees, creating support processes related to service employees, creating support processes related to IT. It is important to keep customer at the heart of the blueprint. This will help in bringing the customer view of the processes and standards in the blueprint leading to a more effective blueprint.

Physical Evidence	Website	Branch	Teller Window	Computer	Card Machine		Fun Request	Signature
Customer actions	Arrives at Bank	Security Check	Waits in line	Makes request to Teller	Provides ID	Swipes Card	Waits	Request Completed
Onstage contact actions	Greets Customer	Confirms Customer Identity	Receives Request	Provides necessary forms and information	Acquires money		Request is fulfilled	
Backstage contact actions		Assists with new accounts and applications		Processing Deposits	Accessing funds for withdrawal			
Support Processes	Running Website	Cleaning the grounds		Restocking forms			Guiding customer to teller	

Figure 2.4 Blueprint for a services marketing system

The key steps in developing the blue print are:

1. Identification of main activities in developing and providing service;
2. Defining the "big picture" prior to "drilling down" to get a detailed view;
3. Distinguishing "front stage" and "backstage";
4. Clarification of interactions among customers, employees, and supportive backstage actions and systems;
5. Identification of points that are likely to fail; development of precautionary procedures; preparation of exigency plans;
6. Development of criteria for activity implementation—task completion time, maximum wait time, and scripts to guide communications between employees and customers.

Conclusion

The chapter starts with the identification of distinctive characteristics of financial products and how can organizations tackle with them. The chapter then moves through the consumer decision-making process and conceptualizes the financial product as a unique service product where concepts related to service encounter, service script, and service blueprint have been introduced to manage satisfactory firm customer interactions for a financial company. The role of culture and how to deal with misbehaving customers also has been dealt with in detail in this chapter. The author closes with a framework for customer satisfaction in the purchase journey of financial products. The key takeaways of this chapter are:

- Distinctive service-related features of financial products.
- Consumer decision-making process.
- Managing the service encounter.
- Dealing with misbehaving customers.
- The impact of culture on financial products.
- Designing the service blueprint and script for financial products companies.

CHAPTER 3

Managing Customer Expectations

Chapter Overview

Customer expectations are the building blocks of customer satisfaction. Chapter 3 discusses the role of customer expectations and how they are formed in detail for financial products. It then talks about how financial companies can play a role in setting realistic customer expectations. The chapter concludes by discussing ways to manage customer expectations with reference to financial products in detail. The role of physical settings and ambience is also explained through the concept of servicescapes.

Role of Customer Expectations in Marketing Financial Products

To achieve customer satisfaction and delight companies today need to learn and manage customer expectations. In financial products since it is only the delivery that can be seen expectations related to that becomes important. Customer expectations in relation to service delivery are views about service delivery that a customer believes he or she would get and is a measure of service's performance (Zeithaml and Bitner 2000). Therefore, customer expectations act as reference points and with the help of these points, customer assesses the perceptions of performance regarding service. Knowledge about customer expectations is vital for a financial marketer.

Two Levels of Customer Expectations and Zones of Tolerance

Through their exploratory research, Zeithaml and Bitner (2000) have quoted that expectations vary from customers to customers regarding service, the same is true in case of financial products also. The first level is called the "Desired Level." This is the service level, customer expects to get or wish, and believes that this can be achieved. The following example illustrates this.

Naresh is a company executive in his 30s. He is married with two kids. His work profile is very demanding as it is a client service function and he always seems to be pressed for time. He plans to buy an insurance policy but is not able to take out time for completing the procedures. He is looking for an insurance agent who could assist him in this and take care of all the formalities. Naresh is also ready to pay a price for this service. Through this example it becomes clear that even in a product like insurance there is a need for servicing where the client is ready to pay fees. However, there happened to be a conflict in Naresh's wished for or desired level of expectation with reference to this expectation. The agents available in the market had been asking 15x the fees he was ready to pay as the right price; he was ready to go up to 2x. Thus "x" was the desired or wished-for level of fees, whereas adequate level of fees was "2x."

"Adequate Level" of service is the lower level of expectation—the level at which the customer will accept. Customers not only wish for the desired level but also recognize that they may not be able to get that level and settle down at the minimum expected level, which is the adequate level of service expectation.

Customers evaluate service performance on the basis of two levels of expectations: desired and adequate. Because of the heterogeneity in financial services delivery performance can vary from one encounter to another with the same employee, across different employees from the same provider and across different providers. Customers are ready to accommodate this difference to a certain extent, which is known as the "zone of tolerance" (Zeithaml and Bitner 2000). This tolerance zone comes between the desired and adequate levels (Figure 3.1). When service is below adequate level, the customer will not accept the product and when the service is above desired level then he/she may be delighted if that criterion is important to him/her. In Naresh's case, if fees is above 2x he would not hire the service and if it is less than x then he would be delighted. The zone of tolerance varies under different conditions. The desired level,

Desired Level
Tolerance Zone
Adequate Level

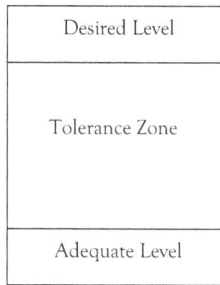

Figure 3.1 Tolerance zone

which can be considered as the maximum level, also may be similar but the minimum level that is adequate level may vary from customer to customer across the industry. Different individuals will have different zones of tolerance. This would result in some customers for a financial products organization having narrower zones and some may have expanded zones. Contrary to Naresh on his expectation for time, Radhavallabh, who is 65 years old and has time on his side, does all the office-related procedures with his policy himself and is not even prepared to pay the x price also.

Zones of Tolerance Differ for Different Service Attributes

Within the financial product a customer may be looking for multiple attributes such as returns, security, credibility, and so on. On each of the attribute, customer would have expectations. For every expectation there would be a zone of tolerance. Attributes that are more important for the customer will have tighter zones of tolerance, whereas the less important ones would have a wider tolerance zone. Figure 3.2 displays the tolerance zone of a bank deposit customer. The return is a more important attribute than the friendliness of the employee so the zone of tolerance for the rate of return on the deposit is smaller for him.

It has also been observed that the tolerance zones would fluctuate between the first service expectation and the expectation of recovery. If the previous expectation has been satisfactory the customer would have a wider zone of tolerance for service recovery, but if the first time service interaction turns negative the customer will have a tighter zone of tolerance for service recovery. Similarly, zone of tolerance for a process

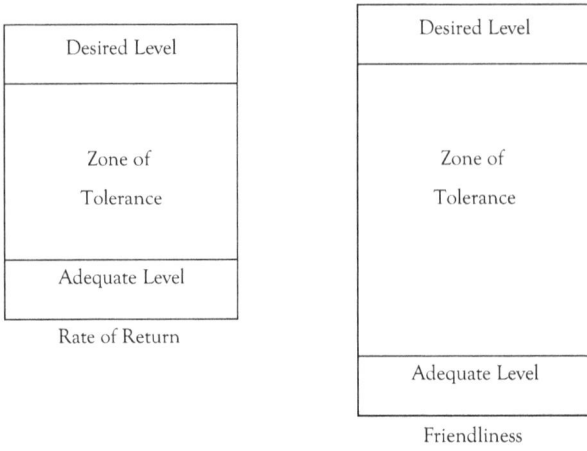

Figure 3.2 Tolerance zones of two separate service product attributes

dimension of delivery would be wider than the outcome dimension. Desired level is normally more stable than the adequate level, which is dependent more on the external fluctuations. Competition is also a significant factor in it.

Given the importance of customer expectations in a financial product, marketers must have knowledge about them along with the knowledge of how to have control over them. This would require them to understand how expectations are formed. Figure 3.3 illustrates a framework for

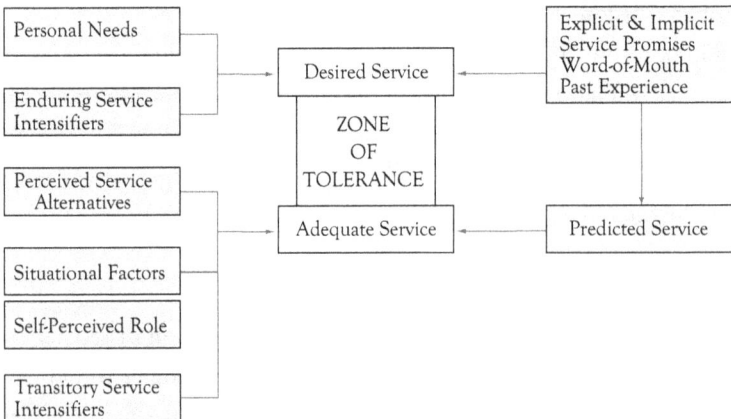

Figure 3.3 A framework for customer expectations

* *Source:* Zeithaml and Bitner 2000.

customer expectations. The starting point would be the factors related to the personal needs. Personal needs include factors that are essential for the psychological and physical well-being of the customer. These could be physical, functional, social, and psychological.

Enduring service intensifiers cover factors that are more stable in nature and can lead to the customers heightened sensitivity to the service act. For example, a young insurance customer in his 30s would want the maximum life cover for his family members. Since age is on his side he can bargain on that for the maximum cover and taking care of the family is his/her personal need. This is illustrated in Figure 3.4. A person's underlying generic attitude and meaning on a service attribute becomes his personal service philosophy and is also a source of enduring service intensifier. When a customer follows direction and instructions, he believes that the firm would also do so and does not expect time deviations to happen in the service delivery.

Customer's approach is an important factor that affects the personal need. For example, one company obtains a health insurance from a renowned insurance broking organization. The company wants the broker to explain its employees' behavior related to health to the insurance service provider. In order to do this, the broker should have deep insights of the employees' health behavior of his/her client company. That way, the broker can negotiate the price and would get an overall picture of the

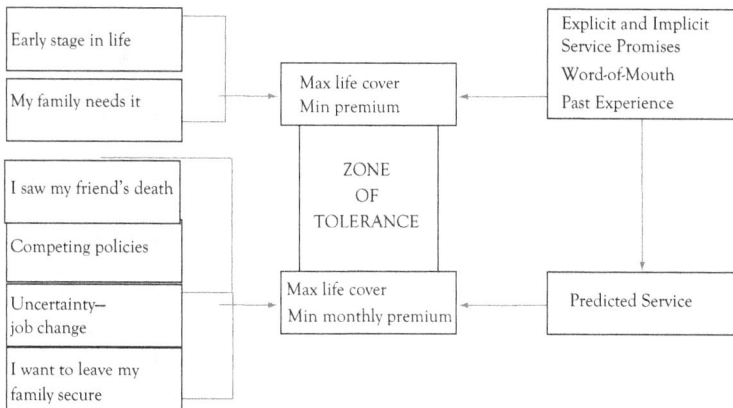

Figure 3.4 Zone of tolerance for an insurance customer on need for the product attribute

employees' health behavior to live up to the customer expectation. The implicit approach behind the expectation is clear.

Five factors determine the adequate expectation's level of customers (Zeithaml, Berry and Parasuraman 1993). These need to be understood by the marketer to arrive at satisfied customers. Transitory service intensifiers are of momentary type; however, they generate intensified expectation at a particular point in time. An accident patient would want the health insurance company to be extremely quick to respond to his call for insurance. The service expectation also asks for empathy in behavior of the insurance company's employees. The zone of tolerance becomes very narrow because of this temporary emergency.

Perceived service alternative is one more factor that has an influence over the adequate level of service expectation. It is a customer's judgment regarding several alternatives, which can meet his expectation. If alternative services are increasingly available, then the adequate level of service expectation would be on the upper side. In contrast, if a customer has fewer options, that customer would accept what is available or presented to him/her. When there are no alternatives, a health policyholder agrees for lesser amount against claims for reimbursement. This brings down the adequate service level and widens the tolerance zone.

The third factor that shapes up the customer expectation at the adequate level is the customer's self-perceived service role. As discussed in Chapter 2 through the role and script theory, customers and employees are actors in a service performance. A customer of a financial products company therefore has a part in the service expectations. In instances where service recipient's role is obvious, there would be high expectation. Let's say, a health policyholder knows clearly what he or she should expect from a service provider and fulfills all its requirements. In that situation, the tolerance zone shrinks as the customer has very high expectations. On the contrary, a health policyholder who does not conform to the service provider's requirement and does not follow his or her self-perceived role; in such case, the expectation level is low and tolerance zone naturally expands.

Situational conditions also act as a factor that influences adequate level of customer expectation. Upon getting an understanding by a customer that certain situational factors are not in the hands of the service provider, the zone of tolerance widens. Of late, instances of COVID-19 pandemic describe this factor in a nice manner. People were aware that going to banks and ATMs is conducive to the spread of the virus so they switched to electronic transactions. To complete this they would try to finish the transactions early morning, which otherwise would be done any time in the day. Thus, their zone of tolerance with reference to time of the bank service widened. However, if a customer contacted corona virus and his condition deteriorated, his zone of tolerance for the insurance provider decreases with reference to the time taken in servicing his request for hospitalization-related claims.

The service level that a customer expects is called as predicted service level. One more factor that affects the expectation of service is this. The predicted service level is set by an earlier experience that the customer may have had with the firm, the word of mouth going around for the firm and the explicit and implicit promises made by the firm through the marketing and corporate communications. An individual would choose a state-run insurance provider because he would believe the firm to be more credible and reliable than the private sector agencies and be ready to invest in its policy. A positive experience will widen his zone of tolerance while a negative experience would narrow it.

Figures 3.4 and 3.5 illustrate the zone of tolerance for an insurance customer for two different attributes; need for insurance product and the customer service required.

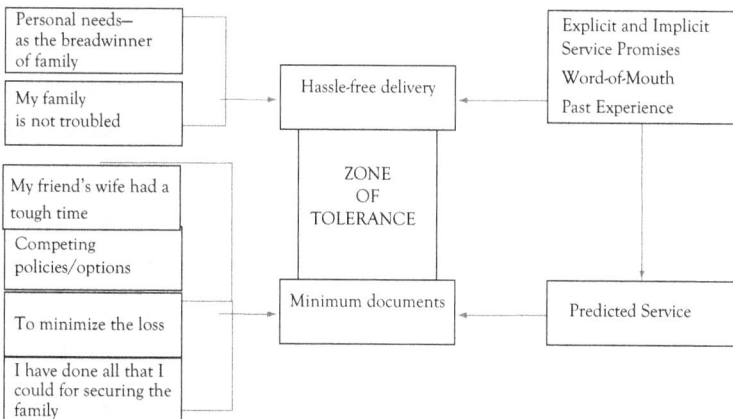

Figure 3.5 Zone of tolerance for an insurance customer on customer service attribute

An idea about the different sources of expectations helps a financial service marketer in understanding the weight of each source in the customer's decision making and how to reach that particular source that could have an influence in customer's decision.

It has been found that many times financial marketers are afraid of asking the customers about their expectations. The fear stems from the fact that they believe that the customer will have unrealistic and extravagant expectations, and by asking for it the company endangers itself for heavier expectations. Contrary to this belief, customer expectations are often very basic and simple. They expect financial products service providers to do what they are meant to and not anything fancy. Table 3.1 illustrates this. Many times customers are frustrated because even the basic service is not provided.

Table 3.1 Customer expectations in financial service products

Type of Financial Organization	Type of Financial Product	Customer Expectation
Bank	Deposit	Keep my money safe (I do not want the bank to invest in loss making ventures or ventures with very high risk). I want reasonable returns (I would expect rate of interest competitive).
	Loan	I want competitive rates (I have searched the market and know the rates of other players). I should feel secure (all dealings and processes must assure me of the credibility of the bank).
NBFC	Loan	I want better rates (the reason for me to come to an NBFC is lower rates; otherwise I would have gone to a commercial bank).
Insurance	Terms and conditions	Keep me informed all through (do not play underneath the words just to sell).
Mutual Funds	Risk conditions	I understand equity mutual fund would have higher risk (but I still want the returns to be more than the deposit rate of interest in the commercial bank).

Managing Customer Expectations

Instead of not asking the customers about their expectations financial product companies may ask and improvise the processes accordingly. It may not be possible to always incorporate every expectation level of the customer. In such cases, the company needs to inform the customers and if appropriate also explain the reasons of not doing so. The worst thing for a company to do would be to ask and promise on service expectations but not perform. This will result into a negative image and word of mouth along with generating dissatisfied customers. There are ways in which a marketer can influence the sources of customer expectations as indicated in Table 3.2.

Table 3.2 Ways of influencing customer expectations

Factors	Ways of Influencing
Personal Financial Needs	Educate the customers to make them realize their financial needs as per the needs hierarchy. To illustrate an educated independent woman who would need financial independence even at old age.
Enduring Service Intensifiers	Use customer insights generated through research to understand their personal service philosophies and sources of desired expectations. For example, the socioeconomic profile of customers would indicate their need for specific group of financial products.
Perceived Service Alternatives	The knowledge about competitive financial offerings available. For example, a householder with excess income may be able to put his money in savings bank account, insurance policies, mutual funds, or fixed deposit. The service provider must be able to analyze the financial need and compare all alternatives with their pros and cons.
Self-Perceived Customer Role	Inform customer to understand his role in the purchase and consumption of the financial product.
Explicit Service Promises	Give a realistic estimate regarding financial product attributes rather than optimistic. For example, the opening of bank account will take one working day. Train the employees to give information aligned to the financial firm's strategy and as per the service script. Not to engage in promises based on competitor's pricing strategies. Formalize promises in tangible ways like zero balance account.

(Continues)

Table 3.2 (*Continued*)

Factors	Ways of Influencing
Implicit Service Promises	The tangibles to be aligned to the marketing strategy of the financial company. For example, an insurance company promising hassle-free delivery must have office spaces designed that are open and integrated i.e., hassle free.
Word of Mouth Communications	To enable the existing satisfied customers to give testimonials and advocate the brand.
Transitory Service Intensifier	A catastrophe or earthquake may create a peak in demand for insurance and other financial products that may have to be liquidated. Financial firms must make a provision for those.
Past Experience	Customer data for previous experiences may inform about the customer lifestyle, product-related terms and preferences, which can be used to better the next service experience.
Situational Factors	Scope for divergence and exception to be kept in the service delivery that can be accommodated by staff toward service recovery. For example, many times private companies allow agents to give discounts on insurance and hence reduce the premiums.
Predicted Service Level	Inform customers of a realistic standard for the product and associated service terms so that expectations also remain realistic.

Underpromising may not only help reduce the gap between expectations and perception but also lose the competitive appeal of an offering. Sometimes customer expectation would be self-fulfilling and his perceptions may start falling below it, thus underpromising has to be exercised with caution.

Apart from the communication to manage customer expectations it may be important for a marketer to design the spaces as per the waiting lines' psychology.

Psychology of Waiting Lines

As noted by David Maister (1984) in his article, "The Psychology of Waiting Lines," it has been observed many times that: "waiting is frustrating, demoralizing, agonizing, aggravating, annoying, time consuming and incredibly expensive." This truth is applicable in financial service encounters as well. Even when a service encounter is efficient, considerate, and comprehensive, the time required to get the provider's attention alters the overall judgments of customers regarding the quality of service. He mentioned that though the mathematical theory of waiting lines (or queues) had been discussed in scholarly research with successful application of their findings, the larger part of this work related to objective reality resulting in different "queuing techniques," which are used in designing the service operations in a financial organization from the technical point have not been researched. These include application questions such as what was the average waiting times' effects of adding servers, on the "queue discipline" that is, the serving order of customers, speeding up serving time, and so on. In financial service encounters, since the experience is subjective when present in a physical facility, there is a need for managers to be concerned about the waiting times of their customers. It is not the actual waiting time but the feelings and emotions associated that create the wait to seem long or short. Maister in his article has explained the waiting lines' psychology, that is, investigated about the experience of waits. He has raised several propositions that would help practicing managers to change the waiting experience of customers. He starts by stating the two laws of service that are applicable to financial organizations as well. The first law of service is stated by the formula S=P–E. S denotes customer satisfaction, P is perceived level of service, and E stands for expected level of service. According to this formula, a customer will be satisfied when the perceived level of service received is greater than the expected level and be dissatisfied if it is vice versa. Expectation as well as perception is not reality, rather they are psychological phenomena and only have some association with reality. This is why purely objective measures may not be very fruitful. Financial marketers must be attentive to the facts such as:

i. What they really did for a customer?
ii. What did a customer perceive?

The second law of service given by Maister is:
"It's hard to plan catch-up ball."

Therefore, in case a manager plans to contribute time and/or money in making services better, it is better to do it in the nascent stage only. The chapter discusses about eight propositions that are detailed as follows.

Proposition 1: Occupied time feels shorter than unoccupied time.
Solution proposed: Sidetrack and/or provide an advantage.

Many times people standing in queues get bored because of being aware of the passage of time and not doing anything. A good strategy for a financial products company could be to distract and/or provide an advantage. For instance: Over a packed cashier's desk, customers who are waiting to be served could be sent to passbook entry or to the ATM, others for cash withdrawal and so on, and can be given forms to fill. It also needs to be checked that the activities inserted to cover up the waiting time should be advantageous and relevant to the customer in some way or the other.

Proposition 2: An in-process wait feels less long than a preprocess wait.
Solution proposed: The system should acknowledge the entry of a customer.

It is also observed that many times a customer has to wait for long before his turn comes up for actual transaction in a financial organization. It would be good if the company acknowledges the entry of the customer in the system. This can be done by greeting the customer and giving a number for his turn either by a receptionist or a machine and informing him the expected time of the wait. It also gives a sense to the customer that the process has started as people want to get started in a process rather than sitting idle.

Proposition 3: Anxiety makes waits seem longer.
Solution proposed: Understand what worries the customers in line and resolve it (no matter what, rational or irrational).

Most of the times when people are in queues it seems that "The other line always moves faster" and this creates anxiety because of which the wait becomes intolerable. It would be good to understand this by the marketer so that there is somebody who through his friendly gestures is approachable by the customers and can resolve their queries. It can be replaced by technology although face-to-face contact may be more relational for the customer to open up.

Proposition 4: Known is better than unknown when it comes to waiting time.
Solution proposed: Tell honestly the waiting time.

The most intense basis of anxiety in waiting is around the duration of the wait, that is, how long the wait will be. Many times people suffer from an appointment syndrome. In this, people arrive earlier than the time of appointment and are ready to wait till the scheduled appointment time, but any time beyond that even a short amount can unnerve them. It is good if the customers are informed about the delay and the expected amount of time to wait.

Proposition 5: Less explanation, longer the wait feels.
Solution proposed: Early explanations and more updates.

Customers are ready to wait with much more patience for a process to take place in a financial products company if they are explained with the details of the wait, as this eases their anxiety and idle time.

Proposition 6: Higher the unfairness, longer the wait feels.
Solution proposed: Promote and practice fairness while serving customers.

Customers get furious when they see people cutting the line. It is important for the financial manager to monitor the line and not let this happen. The other thing that can be done is to serve customer as per a rule that should be known to the customer such as "First come First serve." If there is no order maintained, every customer standing in the line is not relaxed but always highly tensed and nervous so that his turn may not be taken away and no unfair serving to customers be done.

Proposition 7: More value, more wait.
Solution proposed: Segregate customers, increase speed at nonvalue-addition process points.

A customer with a high lifetime value can be considered a premium customer and served on priority by another team. Also withdrawals and other services can be automated so that fast transactions may happen.

Proposition 8: Time does not fly when waiting alone in a line rather than in a group.

Solution proposed: Encourage communication among customers waiting in a line.

It is seen many times that individuals waiting in a line in a branch do not talk or interact with each other. But if a delay happens or there occurs a fault in serving the queue they start talking to each other in despair. If the service marketer recognizes this behavior, provision for interaction can be made in the way waiting area is designed. The reason for this is that people find comfort in waiting in groups rather than alone.

Proposition 9: Solo waits feel longer than group waits.
Solution proposed: Promote a sense of group waiting.

It has been seen often that individuals sitting or standing next to each other in a waiting line without talking or otherwise interacting suddenly start talking when the announcement of a delay is made. They collectively wonder around what is happening, and console each other highlighting the fact that there is some comfort in groups. The more people engage with each other, the less they notice the wait time. In fact, in some situations, waiting in line is part of the experience.

Exceeding Customer Expectations

Often marketing managers across financial institutions talk about exceeding customer expectations. While laying down the strategy of the firm, management needs to deeply think about this. Exceeding expectations is possible when the firm has underpromised or as an exception. Rather honoring promises is the key to satisfied and loyal customers. Alternatively, companies practicing customer relationship management can use customer information to customize their product and give personalized attention to the customer.

Mr. H. S. Bhati, manager of the Punjab National Bank Sukhrali, Gurugram Branch in Haryana, India, makes it a point to note the mobile numbers of all its premium customers. Whenever a new plan arrives he would check on the profile of the customer and make a personal call to him/her informing about the offer and asking their choices, preferences, and interest. Customers become more familiar with the bank's products and processes and can make a call to him more comfortably as a friend than a new bank, which seems like a stranger.

The Role of Integrated Marketing Communication in Managing Customer Expectations

The multimedia environment of today has made information ubiquitous to all across different platforms: traditional and digital. As indicated in the framework of customer expectations marketing communications are a central source of influencing customer expectations. The customer of a financial products organization gets two types of marketing communications: external and interactive. External marketing communications comprises promotion of sales, publicity, digital platforms, public relations, and advertising. Interactive communications in marketing involve messages that customers get from the employees: personal selling, customer service, physical settings, and personal web pages and social media pages of employees. There is a third type of marketing communication that happens within the organization: internal marketing communications comprising of vertical and horizontal communications. There is a need to maintain consistency across all these channels by the company. Most of the times, a failed service experience happens because of a gap in the external service promises done by the company and actual service delivery experienced by the customer. There could be overpromising or lack of requisite information on service delivery by the customer, which will affect the perceived level of service by the customer. Thus, it becomes significant for the marketer to have knowledge about the factors that may lead to such problems. The factors are:

i. Inadequate management of service promises;
ii. Raised expectations of customers;
iii. Lacking enough education of customers;
iv. Scarce internal communications.

The following section will deal with each one of the problems and the ways to manage them.

Inadequate Management of Service Promises

When financial product companies are not able to meet the promises made by the sales people, service employees, and advertising in their service delivery, a gap occurs between them and the customer. This is due to the reason that company does not have the necessary information and integration to fulfill the promises. Many a time there is a tendency to mis-sell by the sales people in the financial product companies. Sometimes the traditional functional structure also acts as a deterrent.

Raised Expectations of Customers

It is the responsibility of both operations and marketing to make accurate and appropriate information available to the customer. It is desirable that marketing should interestingly show actual scene of service transactions and service operations should deliver as promised.

Lacking Enough Education of Customers

Many times differences in service delivery promises happen when financial companies do not adequately instruct their customers. If the customers are not clear about their role in service delivery, the nature of service delivery, or do not understand how to assess services, they may often be disappointed and feel that the financial company is responsible and not they themselves. Inexperienced customers may not know how to use the service. Financial products being high credence services may perplex the customer as they do not understand the criteria on which to assess and do not have technical expertise; similarly, long duration of the financial products customers may not understand the complexity involved in the processes. Managers in these companies should not assume that through one or two interactions or some provision of information the customers will know it all. This is one of the reasons for customers to defect.

Scarce Internal Communications

It is worthy that the multiple functions in a financial organization should be coordinated. There are different departments and service employees involved in the discharge of various roles. This is to be done to secure an organization structure in place, but the customer is not interested in either the organization structure or the hierarchy. Thus, the design of the organization should be customer centric so that all departments are well coordinated to attain the target of service provision and customer satisfaction.

To match service promises to service delivery financial institutions may adopt four different strategies. These are:

- Managing promises of service;
- Dealing with expectations of customers;
- Educating customer;
- Managing internal marketing communication.

Managing promises of service include:

Giving clear information—The information given has to create a clear impression about the financial company and its service in the minds of the customer.

Employ visual imagery—A visual image is easier to recall and remember. Financial products company must try to illustrate the concept, product, or brand by using visuals, which could also be the brand name and logo in their communication.

Highlight the tangibles—Since financial products are intangibles, using tangibles associated with the products and the company give a sense of comfort and ease the customers. Thus tangibles should be used in the promises being made.

Exhibit service employees in message—Service employees are the physical and human aspects of the financial products and can cater to the emotional and psychological needs of the customers. They also help in building relationships on the ground and thus they can be used in the service-related communications.

Promise real—As already highlighted, making high or low expectations would create difficulty for financial marketer and service promises should be made at the level that customers realistically expect them to achieve.

Encourage verbal communication—Because of the experiential nature of the product individuals refer to someone in their network to get a sense of the company, its product and service. Positive word of mouth much more than paid communications such as advertising and financial companies must encourage customers to exchange positive notes. They may also use customer testimonials in the paid communications.

Furthermore, companies in financial products sector must coordinate among all physical, digital, and human points of paid and unpaid external communications and introduce service guarantees on the features of their product concept, which may be unique and important to the customers. These may not necessarily relate to the core product terms but could be on supplementary services as well.

Dealing With Expectations of Customers

There are times when the terms and conditions of financial services change over time. It is not possible to offer the customers the same as before and it becomes difficult for the customer to expect. It is worthwhile to consider offering customers options and reset expectations in such conditions. With this giving of choice the client does not feel cheated, the change is communicated slowly and gradually, and he also gets a feeling of respect with reference to the financial products company. This kind of communication decreases the chances of customer leaving the company. Tiered offerings based on the value of the customer are also one good option and is practiced by many financial organizations. Over the course of the service experience the interaction with the financial firm will also establish criteria to assess the firm's performance and quality, thus managing customer expectations. Marketers in a financial organization also need to polish their negotiation skills so that unrealistic expectations are dealt with.

Educating Customers

It has been emphasized earlier that customers perform service roles in financial products. It is thus important for the financial marketers to educate them of their roles in the process by giving adequate information. Financial organizations also need to take care that their product performance is communicated to the customer in friendly terms that he can understand. Only then can the customer evaluate the effectiveness of the service provider's performance. The organizations also need to understand the different customer roles in the decision-making process. While wife may not be the decision maker for an investment option in some Indian households, she still can be a strong influencer to her husband who is the decision maker. Thus, informing and convincing her is also important for a financial products agent regarding an investment decision. With a relationship developing between the financial services organization and a customer, any development and information related to risk and benefits is to be relayed to the customer in a personal and friendly manner by the financial products manager.

Managing Internal Marketing Communication

Financial organizations must see how information needs to be provided to the customer contact employees along with the tools, techniques, and skills to perform well in interactive marketing communication between them and the customer. Training, human resource practices, and downward vertical communications would help in building these. The employees also have to see that they check the company's advertising and selling communications along with digital mediums so that they are aware of what is being communicated outside and be updated on the same. In the absence of this, a gap may occur between employees and customers and the performance would be impacted negatively. Also, upward communications from customers facing employees must travel the management hierarchy of a financial service organization so that no customer-related issue goes unheard.

Along with managing the vertical communications, it is important that the channels of communication between marketing and operations department remain open. This will help both the departments as operations would know what the advertising has talked about and keep in mind during service delivery. Similarly, external marketing communications can take actual service employees performing their roles in the advertisements. Further sales and operations also need to keep their communication channels open so that they know where the gaps happen on the ground and can correct that. There also has to be integration between back-office processes and employees with the front-office processes and employees. Cross-functional teams can also be made to achieve integration between employees across departments.

While designing strategies to manage customer expectations, the financial products company essentially needs to convey the significance of knowing and understanding what the customer expects and deliver accordingly. This should not be seen as a mere tactic; it is in essence the first step of value creation for the customer. Oftentimes, human acts and emotions that show care, understanding, and empathy create customer stickiness.

Designing the Servicescape

Physical evidence or tangible cues often become the basis of assessing a service product by the customer. Aesthetics and physical proof is a vital aspect of prepurchase and postpurchase satisfaction of the customer. The elements of physical evidence has to be taken care of by a financial organization that is, the exterior, interior, and other tangibles features of a premise/facility. The exterior of a premise comprises the architecture, the outer design, car parks, signage, and neighboring milieu. The interiors include inner architectural designs, paraphernalia, signage, floor plan, temperature, and quality of air. Besides, the additional tangibles consist of cards, stationery, bills, reports, uniforms, brochures, Internet/web/social media pages, and so on. Bitner (1992) coined the term "servicescape." She explained that servicescape is the physical milieu where business transactions (including provision of services) of an organization of service sector takes place; it includes several elements as hue, music, fragrance, furniture, floor plan, and so on. The elements of servicescape either facilitate the service transaction or communicate something about the organization. It is now known that the design of the physical environment has an effect on consumer expectations, choices, behaviors, and satisfaction, and also on employee motivation, productivity, and satisfaction. In deciding the design of the servicescape in a financial services organization three things need to be considered:

- People who would be placed in the servicescape;
- Organizational goals to be met and the role of servicescape in it;

- The degree of complexity involved in the process using servicescape.

The servicescape acts as a package for the financial products. Whether physical or electronic, the environment wraps the service product and gives an impression of what would be available inside. It thus acts as the **package**. The servicescape also acts as the **facilitator** in helping customers and employees discharge their roles. The efficiency of design would inhibit or enhance the flow of service activities making it easy for customers and employees. The **socialization** process is also aided by the servicescape. It conveys the roles and behavior of employees and customers and associations among them. Finally, the servicescape acts as a differentiator many times for the financial organizations. When products have similar terms, conditions, and returns in the market, then servicescape acts as a facilitating service, offering competitive advantage to such organizations.

The effects of the servicescape on human behavior can be understood through the stimulus response theory. The servicescape is considered as the stimulus, individuals (employees and customers), and their behaviors targeted at the environment as responses. The underlying hypothesis is that customers and employees will react in a particular manner to the dimensions of servicescape. The internal reactions of individuals would comprise cognitive, emotional, and physiological responses that would lead to individual behaviors and social interactions between the customers and the employees. Figure 3.6 details the framework.

Individuals normally react to a place as either avoidance or affiliation. Affiliation would include all positive behaviors, for example, wish to work, associate, stay, and explore. The behaviors associated with avoidance would be the opposite of these. Along with these responses the servicescape can also aid satisfaction of a consumer goal for visiting the organization. Together with this it is known that social interactions happen within a physical container and that is where the servicescape affects the quality of customers' interactions and its nature. There are times where a satisfied or dissatisfied customer employee interaction creates a spiral effect on subsequent interactions. The reason is that customer satisfaction is actually influenced by his perceptions of service environment.

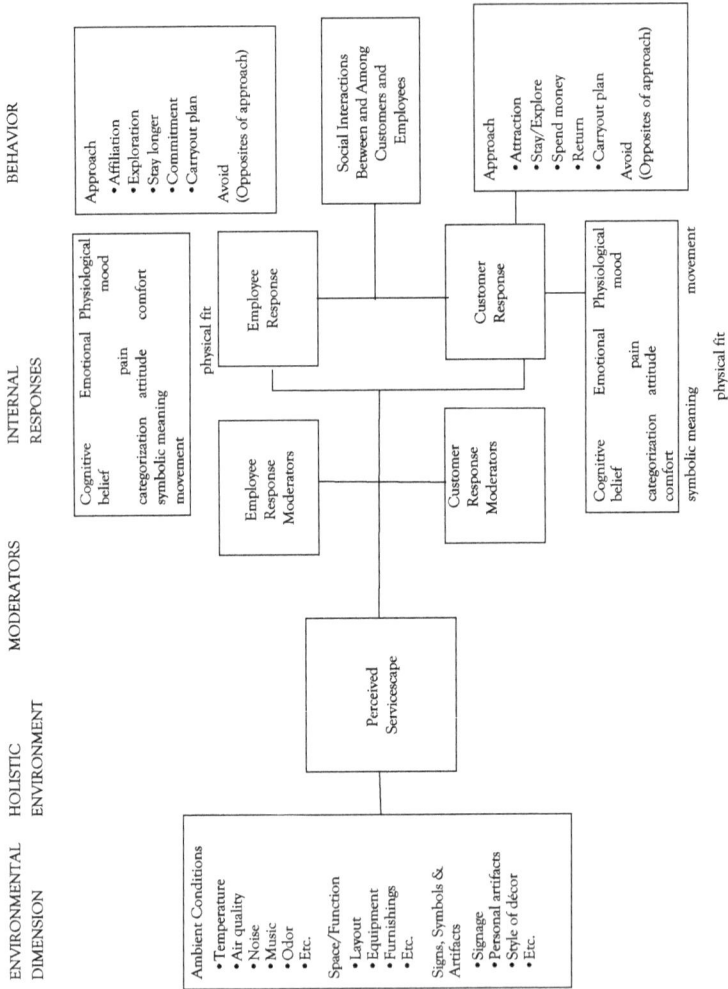

Figure 3.6 **The servicescape framework**

Source: Zeithaml and Bitner 2000.

Thus servicescape helps in elucidating the service rules, expectations, and conventions in a given service context.

Harris and Goode (2010) conceptualized e-servicescape as consisting of three dimensions: online layout and functionality, aesthetic appeal, and financial security. Two dimensions from it are rather similar to the original work of Bitner (1992); however, in order to be applicable in an online environment, the third dimension (signs, symbols, and artifacts) is modified to financial security. Web environments' designing entails designing of the virtual site where customers from e-service settings encounter with services so as to have a positive effect on users and could raise positive responses (Dailey 2004). Internet web pages are making significant strides in the commercial arena as an electronic-servicescape, and they are predicted to become more prominent in the approaching period (Lai et al. 2014). Earlier research has shown the impact of environmental cues on purchase intention and website trust (Harris and Goode 2010), trust and relationship building (Papadopoulou et al. 2002), customers' cognitive and affective responses, and specific shopping behaviors in terms of both approach and avoidance outcomes. In their model, Harris and Ezeh (2008) conceptualized the link between offline servicescape factors and loyalty intention, which Allmér extends in an online environment (2014). The study was empirically evaluated in the field of travel and tourist websites, with the proposal that it be expanded to cover other services in the future (Sreejesh and Ponnam 2017).

As per the research evidence, it will help in forming positive attitude about an online shop, assure repeat purchase intention, and promote positive word-of-mouth publicity, consequently, would create a better image of shop and a reduction in the perceived risk by online customers. Managers who are concerned with the website designing of fashion product, thus, ought to ponder over these e-servicescape dimensions so as to include it in developing online strategies in order to increase loyalty and perceived e-shopping value. Accordingly, online shops should invest in each and every e-servicescape dimensions, specifically, layout and functionality and financial security, which have an intense effect on perceived e-shopping value. For gaining trust and enhancing the website value, the vendors of fashion products should pay attention to perceived online financial security, to the privacy feature of financial information, and to diverse payment options. In order to increase the value of perceived e-shopping in the fashion product background, online shops should try to enhance the websites usability, manage the information required, modify web pages to satisfy the needs, and facilitate interaction with customers. Moreover, sellers should also focus more on security by safeguarding transactions and customers' sensitive data and transparency about the usage of their data. Even though, according to the study, the aesthetic appeal dimension of e-servicescape does not have substantial effect on perceived e-shopping value, it is better not to overlook this aspect of e-servicescape. That is, visually appealing web pages produce good first impression and could impact risk perception of users. The "aesthetic appeal" dimension's weak effect is due to the perceived "similarity" of several online shops in relation to originality and appearance of web page. Furthermore, around 34 percent of respondents buy from online shops that are organized as auctions, where aesthetic appearance and having fun while buying are not the most important factors. The authors advocate for research into and on all aspects of business-to-consumer communication, especially on the Web, with a focus on customers.

Conclusion

In this chapter, we learned about the importance of customer expectations in achieving customer satisfaction by firms in financial products. These firms can play an active role in not only understanding and meeting customer expectations satisfactorily but also setting them properly. The key takeaways from this chapter are:

   i. Understanding how customer expectations are set.
   ii. Identifying that a customer can have different levels of expectations for different core product and related attributes.
   iii. Developing a zone of tolerance for customer expectations.
   iv. Understanding the psychology of waiting lines.
   v. Identifying ways of managing customer expectations.
   vi. Designing and setting physical facilities for meeting customer expectations.

CHAPTER 4

Customer Perceptions of Financial Service Products, Service Quality, and Customer Satisfaction

Chapter Overview

This chapter builds on customer perceptions of financial service products characteristics, as these impact the final level of customer satisfaction achieved. The chapter builds on the Gaps model as the conceptual model and SERVQUAL as the scale to measure customer expectations and perceptions.

Conceptualizing Perceptions for Customer Satisfaction

To achieve customer satisfaction in financial service products, two constructs have been taken as the main pillars from the works of Parasuraman et al. (1985): customer expectations and perceptions. Expectations have been discussed in detail in Chapter 3. In this chapter, we will explore the role of perceptions because perceptions are a measure of the customer's assessment of the service product. Perception is the process by which individuals receive information through the five senses and assign meaning to it. Expectations act as the reference points for customers for a particular product, and organization and perceptions are the actual assessment of it. The above-mentioned team of researchers, over a course of time, has developed a service quality model, which would bring customer satisfaction and associated benefits. The center of this model is the difference between customers' perceptions and expectations, which is referred to as the customer gap. Ideally all financial firms, especially in a competitive environment, will want to close this gap. To close this gap, the model suggests closing any/all of the provider gaps that may exist as shown in Figure 4.1.

The four provider gaps would be the basic reasons for creating the customer gap.

- **Provider Gap 1:** Not knowing what customers expect.
- **Provider Gap 2:** Not selecting the right service designs and standards.
- **Provider Gap 3:** Not delivering to service standards.
- **Provider Gap 4:** Not matching performance to promises.

Any financial institution, in order to acquire and retain customers, must reduce the customer gap. This would entail implementing a system of monitoring and reviewing the marketing strategy continuously. The results of which would show if there is a gap occurring in any of the provider gaps.

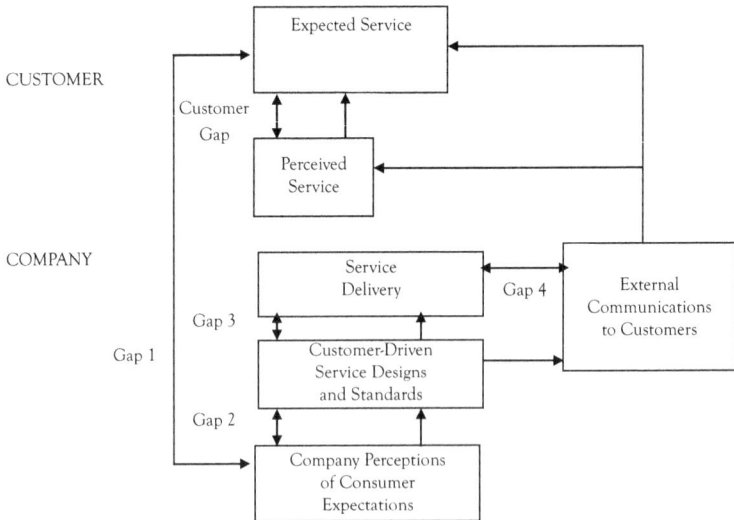

Figure 4.1 Gaps model

Source: Parasuraman 1985.

With appropriate metrics, it can be found out if the company's understanding of expectations is aligned with the actual expectations, whether the design of service processes is around customer-centric standards, if there is a default in performing to set the standards and also assessing if the external promises did not match with what was being delivered. The following example would illustrate the Gaps model.

The financial organization would accordingly decide the marketing strategy based on the 7Ps: processes, people, price, physical evidence, product, place, and promotion. Financial organizations have to be thoroughly aware of the fact that perceptions of customers are compared in relation to expectations. The dynamic nature of expectations varies with time and culture. In the Gaps model, the gap is measured on service quality dimensions. The authors have defined service quality as a multidimensional construct comprising empathy, tangibles, assurance, reliability, and responsiveness. The service quality here does not cover the product quality but only the quality of delivery in service products; that is, it does not tackle the "what" aspect, which relates to the technical quality of the product but only deals with the "how" aspect or functional service quality (Grönroos 1984). The dimensions as defined by the authors are given as follows.

- **Reliability**: Capacity to give accurate and dependable services as promised to customers.
- **Assurance**: Employee's knowledge and consideration and their power to instill confidence and trust.
- **Tangibles**: Infrastructure, amenities, employee's look and appearance.
- **Empathy**: Providing personalized attention and consideration to customers.
- **Responsiveness**: Readiness to help and serve quickly to customers.

The authors also generated a multi-item scale to measure these dimensions as given in the following. Each item was measured both for customer expectation and perception on a 7-point Likert scale (strongly disagree to strongly agree). The difference between perception and expectation was taken as the gap in those items, which the company needs to decide if it is important for the customer and would want to improve.

In highly competitive industries such as financial products, the functional service quality forms a key competitive advantage that can lead to customer stickiness, loyalty, and engagement.

The SERVQUAL items are given as follows:

Reliability

- Giving service as assured;
- Reliability in managing customers' service issues;
- Performing services right the first time;
- Offering services on or before the promised time;
- Preserving flawless records.

Assurance

- Boosting customers' confidence by employees;
- Ensuring safe transactions of customers;
- Reliable courteous employees;
- Knowledgeable employees who can answer customer questions.

Tangibles

- Contemporary equipment;
- Aesthetically pleasing facilities;
- Immaculate, professional appearance of employees;
- Aesthetically pleasing things connected with the service.

Empathy

- Providing personal attention to customers;
- Care and concern from employees for customers;
- Works in the best interest of customers;

- Customers' needs understanding employees;
- Suitable business hours.

Responsiveness

- Preinformation regarding the performance of service;
- Quick service to customers;
- Enthusiasm to assist customers;
- Promptness in responding to customers' requests.

It has been noted by researchers that service quality along with product quality and price leads to satisfaction among customers (Grönroos 1984). The situational and personal factors of the customer also affect customer satisfaction. As defined by Oliver (2006) "Customer satisfaction can be seen as a fulfillment response. It is a judgment that a product or a service feature, or the product or service itself, provides a pleasurable level of consumption related fulfillment." Thus customer satisfaction could be taken as the outcome of the evaluation of a product or service by a customer in regards to the expectations he or she had. Financial products being pure service are largely evaluated by customers on service quality (how the service is delivered) along with product quality (core product benefits).

Managing Customer Perceptions

More factors influence customers than that can be considered. Customers' perceptions of a service product or brand are their thoughts, feelings, and beliefs about it. People make hasty purchases of goods and services. It's difficult to change one's mind once it's formed. As a result, it's critical to cultivate positive consumer views in order to keep your brand in customers' good graces. The following section explains how to construct, improve, and affect it.

Giving Evidence of Service

Since financial products would be intangible in nature, customers would often search for physical cues in every service encounter that they have with financial organizations. Firms would have to build these through the three additional elements of the marketing mix, that is, people, processes, and physical evidence. People include service employees and customers. Physical evidence would include servicescape, technology, guarantees, and any tangible communication. Processes would contain the operational flow of activities and steps in the process.

Measuring Satisfaction of Customers and Quality of Service

Measurements of satisfaction of customers and quality of service has to be done on a regular basis by financial organizations as the customer-centric approach calls for regular monitoring and supervision to identify any problems that may have happened in delivering to the customers, track trends, and integrate customer-focused strategies.

Target Customer Quality and Satisfaction in Every Service Interaction

Every service interaction as a unit corresponds to customer satisfaction and thus retention. The goal of financial companies is to achieve zero defects, thereby achieving hundred percent satisfaction. For this, a clear blueprint would help in establishing the processes along with due documentation done for implementation. Next, a sound understanding of customer expectations needs to be there for every service encounter. These mean scenarios for different types of customers along their buyer journeys need to be mapped with the blueprints by the financial companies. Accordingly, actions for building customer satisfaction have to be elaborated at every customer contact point.

Apart from these, the organizations will need to implement an effective service recovery system in place, along with facilitating adaptability, spontaneity, and flexibility.

Identifying Reasons for the Customer Gap in the Gaps Model

Provider Gap 1 (The Knowledge Gap): Ignorance About Customers' Expectations, Wants, and Needs

Insufficient interest in marketing research:

- Not enough marketing research;
- No research pertaining to service quality;
- Poor application of insights from market research.

Dearth of upward communication:

- Absence of communication between customers and management;
- Lack of interaction between managers and contact employees;
- Several layers amidst top management and contact personnel.

Inadequate focus on relationship:

- Absence of market segmentation;
- Transactions centric instead of relationship centric;
- Attention on new customers in contrast to relationship customers.

Poor service recovery:

- No inspiration to attend to complaints of customers;
- Unable to make changes when things go awry;
- Improper recovery mechanisms in case of service failures.

Provider Gap 2 (The Service Design and Standards Gap): Not Having the Correct Service Designs and Service Standards

Inapt service design:

- Disorganized new service development process;
- Unclear, indefinite service designs;
- Inability to link service design to service positioning.

Lack of customer-driven standards:

- Absence of customer-driven service standards;
- Nonexistence of process management to take care of customer requirements;
- Lack of formal process for setting goals of service quality.

Unfitting physical evidence and servicescape:

- Inability to create tangibles as per customer expectations;
- Servicescape design that does not satisfy employee and customer needs;
- Insufficient maintenance and updation of servicescape.

Provider Gap 3 (The Service Performance Gap): Not Giving in Accord With Service Standards

Lack of human resource policies:

- Unproductive recruitment;
- Conflict and ambiguity over role;
- Poor employee-technology job fit;
- Inapt evaluation and compensation systems;
- Absence of teamwork, empowerment, and perceived control;
- Customers who do not fulfill roles.

Customers who do not know their roles and responsibilities:

- Customers who negatively influence each other;
- Issues with service intermediaries;
- Channel clash over objectives and performance;
- Problem in monitoring quality and consistency;
- Strain between empowerment and control.

Unable to align demand and supply:

- Unable to level the peaks and valleys of demand;
- Unsuitable customer mix;
- Too much dependency on price to even demand.

Provider Gap 4 (The Communication Gap): Nonperformance in Accordance With Promises

Lack of integrated services marketing communications:

- Propensity to consider every external communication as autonomous;
- Not including interactive marketing in communications plan;
- Lack of robust program of internal marketing.

Poor management of customer expectations:

- Lack of customer expectation management in every communication form;
- Absence of sufficient education for customers.

Overpromising:

- Overpromising in advertising;
- Overpromising in personal selling;
- Overpromising through physical evidence cues.

Insufficient horizontal communications:

- Not enough communication between operations and sales;
- Not enough communication between operations and advertising;
- Discrepancies among policies and procedures of all units or branches.

Using Market Research for Managing Customer Expectations and Perceptions

Marketing research assumes an important place in any customer-oriented marketing strategy and that is why it becomes significant in the case of financial products as well. Rather than having a firm-centric view of what customers expect, it is prudent to listen to customer groups for it. The research process though must start with a careful framing of the research problem and the research objectives. This step will help the firm determine its research strategy, which will differ across research problems. For example, does the firm want to understand the customer requirements or assess the customer's response to a new product launch or the reasons for dissatisfaction? A list of indicative research questions is given as follows:

- To understand customer requirements;
- To understand customer expectations;
- To identify causes of service failures;
- To regulate, track, and review service performances;
- To identify reasons of failed service interactions;
- To monitor changing customer expectations.

Research methodologies can be both qualitative and quantitative. Many times there is a need to follow mixed method research where one step of the research process calls for qualitative study and the other for quantitative. To first time understand customer expectations with reference to a new deposit product by a bank, the bank will need to do brainstorming, focus group, and customer panel discussions to identify the same. However, for an established product, a quantitative study is done for monitoring how the bank is doing on those customer-specified criteria.

The research can be done either independently on expectations and perceptions or both taken together for the customers, dependent on the objective. Many times in quantitative studies, there would be a need for testing statistical significance of the associated techniques and variables. It is also many times to be taken care that while administering the SERVQUAL instrument there would be a need to ask customers which service quality dimension among five they consider important. Many times in financial products, reliability is the most significant dimension of service quality for customers. Firms, in such cases, must prioritize for reliability in their marketing strategy (7Ps). Measures of loyalty and the behavioral intentions of customers are also to be included in the research program. The financial organizations must also fix a time interval against which the research would be performed: weekly, fortnightly, monthly, bimonthly, quarterly, half-yearly, and annually. It is also to be looked into if there is an in-house dedicated department to undertake research.

Some of the important research methods that can be used in financial products are given in the following sections.

Customer Complaints Research

In this form of research, all the complaints of the customers are recorded and documented to identify dissatisfied customers and their individual reasons for their dissatisfaction. Wherever possible, the complaint is corrected and also the common points of failure are looked at in detail.

Critical Incident Studies

In these studies, the customer provides the exact account of his/her satisfying or dissatisfying service interactions with the financial products company. These studies are strong and elaborate in getting an understanding of the customer requirements as well. The behavioral insights related to employee performance at the interaction level can be well understood with this method.

Relationship Surveys

This quantitative method is implemented through a structured questionnaire. All significant aspects of the product (price, service quality, and product quality) are raised as questions. Starting with a base year, these surveys can be done annually to track performance and also identify strengths and weaknesses of the financial firm.

Apart from this, financial organizations can conduct post-transaction surveys, hold meeting to understand and review customer expectations, conduct lost customer research, and also do panel research with customer groups.

Managing Service Employees for Customer Satisfaction

The frontline employees or people who are serving customers directly in a financial company and the service employees who support them are important success factors in such an organization. Every person associated with delivering financial product and service would influence the customer's perception of service (Zeithaml and Bitner 2000).

In a service such as insurance, agents become the product and service for the customers. They represent the organization and the brand to the customers and they play the marketers' role in affecting the customer's experience and satisfaction. Research suggests a positive linkage between employee satisfaction, customer satisfaction, and profits. The service climate and well-being of employees are positively correlated with the positive quality perceptions of customers (Schneider and Bowen 1985). The popular concept of service–profit chain (Heskett et al. 1994) highlights significant linkages between employee productivity, internal service quality, and customer value, satisfaction, retention, loyalty, and revenue growth along with profitability. However, there is no causality among employee and customer factors, they just support each other. It is also to be noted that all five dimensions of service quality are actually delivered by employees only.

Of specific mention are the employees who serve the customers at the front end in any financial institutions. These people are actually performing at the periphery of the organization and therefore also referred to as boundary spanners. These people are the link between external customers and internal processes in a financial firm. The jobs these people perform are highly stressful and involve a lot of emotional labor. Often they have to deal with interorganizational and interpersonal conflict and provide trade-offs between firm and customer requirements. Emotional labor goes beyond physical and mental skills required from the employees and includes physical gestures that should be pleasant to the eye such as a smile, expression of interest in the customer's task, conversing in a friendly manner, making eye contact, and so on. The dimensions of service quality—empathy and responsiveness—directly cover these aspects. Irrespective of the mood that the service frontline employee would be in, he/she is expected to keep up the pleasant mannerisms at their desks. Organization's recruitment, selection, and training systems take care of these skills in a boundary spanner. The stress of these employees can be reduced by giving an ambient servicescape, scheduling breaks, rotating positions, and providing support.

There are different kinds of personal or role conflicts faced by boundary spanners. This could be because of a mismatch between their personality traits, values, and orientations. For example, an aggressive person at the front desk in a bank branch is not well aligned to the customer facing roles that has been given to him. The person–job fit theory is a good explanation for this.

Person–Organization or P–O fit is defined as "the compatibility between an individual and a work environment that occurs when their characteristics are well matched" (Kristof-Brown et al. 2005).

P–O fit has different forms. When organizational needs are satisfied by an individual or vice versa, it is called as complementary fit; whereas, when an individual and an organization have analogous characteristics, it is called as supplementary fit (Muchinsky and Monahan 1987). When individuals' personal qualities enable them meeting their organizational demands, they complete their assignments faster and better (e.g., Caldwell and O'Reilly 1990; Hoffman and Woehr 2006; Lauver and Kristof-Brown 2001). This consequently provide them with more time and vigor they require to involve in well-being enhancement activities.

As per the Big 5 personality traits theory, an individual's personality is shaped by the following five traits.

- Extraversion (outgoing/energetic versus solitary/reserved);
- Agreeableness (friendly/compassionate versus critical/rational);
- Openness to experience (inventive/curious versus consistent/cautious);
- Conscientiousness (efficient/organized versus extravagant/careless);
- Neuroticism (sensitive/nervous versus resilient/confident).

Employees who encounter customers (i.e., frontline employees), extraversion, and agreeableness are traits that could be found. Culture affects employee's attitude and behavior. In India, people in formal situations greet each other by joining hands together in contrast to shaking hands. This can cause problem in a financial institution when employees come across people from abroad and they are not comfortable with handshakes. The same applies to females from India. Some people are more comfortable with traditional dress and language. Sometimes there could be problems due to the customer first policy. Owing to the power of customers over employees, problematic customers create issues and lead to conflict. In order to deal with such customers, difficult situations, and minimize conflict, training should be given to employees. Sometimes there are situations, where employee feels that customer is right but management is wrong. In cases like life insurance, where an agent promises a customer on the basis of a policy condition that changes later on; in such situation, agent feels that he/she has wronged the customer. Thus, before the introduction of a change, a financial institution should think about its implications and should introduce it slowly to make its effect less severe and absorbable by agents as well as customers. Another kind of conflict boundary spanners handle is interclient conflict. When there is a discrepancy among demands of clients, like queue jumping, delayed query handling, and so on, the processes need to develop accordingly to handle such discrepancies.

Organizing the Service Employees

To build a strong customer-oriented strong service orientation among the employees, financial institutions need to organize for it. The steps would include the following: hiring the right people matched to the P–O fitment, training and developing employees to be service oriented to the customer, deploying operations that support such culture, and having strategies to retain such people.

It has been observed that in many financial institutions many service employees who face customers are lowest in the corporate hierarchy and have the minimum wages. With the competitive nature of the industry and the advantage derived from a customer-oriented service culture, as described in Chapter 3, recruitment and selection is a critical process where certain criteria matched with the job roles need to be fixed against which candidates are profiled and assessed. It is indeed required to compete for the best people through various placement sources. After identification of suitable candidates, they need to be screened for service competencies and service inclination. Financial organizations may need to have a list of competencies identified and tests either developed or taken from established methods for screening the candidates. A basic personality test can be taken. To hire the best people, it is also required that the financial firm is seen as the preferred employer by the job applicants. Marketing communication tools that are used to talk to the customer are also required to talk to the candidates who would be looking for these jobs.

Sometimes the educational qualification is required as the minimum eligibility condition, but the personality traits become more important to conduct the job. Development officers in insurance companies, while looking for agents, consider the following skills:

- People skills
- Product knowledge
- Self-motivated
- Resilient
- Passionate
- Communication skills
- Good listener

A test can be used to identify the right candidates for the jobs, but it is also important that the development officer has a brand and reputation that such people would want to work for. Once an agent is taken by the development officer, he would need to train him on certain job-specific technical- and communication-related soft skills. The technical skills would include product knowledge and knowledge or practical use of basic computer operations and software. Soft skills would include verbal and nonverbal communication skills, team management, and presentation skills. A new skill that is added to the profile of an insurance agent is social media marketing skill. It is good if the development officer is able to impart these training from the best possible agencies and experts. Training plan has to be a continuous one at regular intervals mapped to the employee growth, performance, career progression, and organizational growth and performance.

Financial organizations also need to empower employees. Empowering employees would mean giving employees the authority to take decision in a specific customer-facing situation. It also includes the requisite desire, knowledge, skills, and tools that the employee must possess to take a decision in a given situation. The organization culture has to show by example how this has to be practiced. Team work is another organizational value that needs to be built in the employees. This would promote integration and smooth flow of activities and processes. Many of the stress-related issues that employees may face can be relieved by such an environment. A step that would help achieve this is that all employees may be seen as serving customers directly even if they are not doing so. This means that they understand their specific job and role, despite them not serving the customer directly. Many times it is possible that employees possess a skill set that can be used in several roles. This would give them a better understanding of the customers from different organizational perspectives and also bring freshness in roles. Job rotation is a practice that many service organizations employ and so can financial organizations. Team-based rewards serve as a good motivational tool for the employees and group rewards would not create ego-related hassles. The support systems, whether from the technology aspect or process aspect, must be robust to help employees perform their roles. Financial organizations may need to measure internal service quality and relationships also. It could be done in the same way as for external customers.

Conclusion

This chapter discusses in detail how to manage customer perceptions to match their expectations for financial products. It details on the Gaps model as an integrated model that can help financial organizations achieve customer satisfaction and provides a detailed view of the SERVQUAL scale. The chapter concludes discussing ways for managing customer perception by financial organizations. The key takeaways from this chapter are:

i. Have conceptual clarity on Gaps model that can be used as an implementation framework and SERVQUAL as a measurement tool for achieving customer satisfaction by financial products firm.

ii. Ways of managing customer perceptions.

CHAPTER 5

Implementing a Relationship-Oriented Service Plan for a Financial Service Product

Chapter Overview

This chapter describes an implementation plan in place for financial institutions to serve the customer and also achieve organizational goals successfully. Through a research study, Srivastava (2004) established a planned process for the same. The steps are presented in the following sections.

A Customer-Oriented Implementation Plan for Financial Organizations

1. It is observed that many times financial organizations start implementing practices and software related to customer relationship management like competitors, just because competitors are doing so. Every financial organization will have a specific and unique charter. It is important that they only adopt a practice if they realize the need for it. While this decision is within the purview of higher management, the need will have to be established through insights received from all levels in the organization. The first point, therefore, would be to relook at the strategic intent of the financial organization (mission and vision). It may be required that these be revisited as per the environmental context.

2. Then the goals have to be defined in a S.M.A.R.T manner:
   • Specific
   • Measurable
   • Achievable
   • Relevant
   • Time bound
3. It would be good to check if the goals formed align to the organizational objectives. The goals have to be specifically measured in a metric, which can be used for analysis including customer-centric metric apart from the regular ones through which financial success of an organization are commonly measured.
4. The above three stages may be seen as critical because it is here where the identity of the financial organization is being crafted, and where there would be uniqueness with respect to other players. All chosen metrics of measurement must be aligned in a meaningful way. Any gap identified may be corrected at this stage and this can be made an annual process.
5. Next the organization resources, competencies, capabilities, and talent need to be screened. Different organizational functions and activities need to be relooked and checked in order to achieve the organizational goals.
6. A monitoring and measuring framework with KPIs defined to be secured in place.

As the financial organization decides to implement a customer-oriented service strategy, they will have to identify customers who can be objectively and subjectively differentiated as high net worth and low-cost individuals. Customer lifetime value can be a good metric to serve the purpose for the financial firms. It can be used for fixing targets for employees. Accordingly, a customer pyramid is generated with different layers. The next decision has to be taken on how to deal with these layers of customers. If the criterion for forming the layers is chosen as income, for example, it has to be seen how these high-income customers be dealt with differently from other layers. The prominent interaction characteristics have to be identified and be made available to the employees who would interact with them. Technology-based systems would play an important role here. Apart from improving the effectiveness, these systems have the ability to make the operational processes more cost effective. However, the most important point is the integration between different systems at a functional level has to be there; otherwise, they become even more tedious than the manual flow of work. The service employees also need to be motivated and trained to interact with the differentiated customer in a particular manner. It is not that only one layer of customer has to be considered. This would depend upon step number 1 to 6.

It is to be highlighted that the management of several financial organizations have discussed about three behavioral customer outcomes that are important for them to achieve. These are "satisfaction," "trust," and "commitment." Depending on the importance given to customer relationships and investments made therein, there could be a direct effect on satisfaction (the attitudinal outcome) and trust (the cognitive outcome). Trust and satisfaction will impact commitment (behavioral outcome). Thus, financial organizations will have to invest in relationships that are centered around the continuous exchange of valued resources by partners. A resource has been defined as everything that gives satisfaction and pleasure as per the social exchange theory (Bagozzi 1975; Holbrook 1999). Interpersonal relationship theories have also talked about resources representing contribution in constructing and preserving relationships (Rusbult 1980; Rusbult and Farrell 1983). Often, consumers build associations with financial organizations that contribute resources in meeting their needs. These investments result in customer outcomes that would include relational characteristics such as trust, commitment, and consumer satisfaction. If consumers perceive that, they get the needed resources from the organization to solve their problems assist in gaining trust. As shown in Figure 5.1, organisations making investments to reduce uncertainty, improve the relationships' effectiveness, and increase efficiency (Gutek et al. 2000) are able to build the customers' trust. Trust leads to commitment and is a vital characteristic of unbeaten associations (Morgan and Hunt 1994). Commitment shows the willingness to remain in a relationship, as it is treasured (Moorman et al. 1992). Financial institutions that devote resources to meet consumer needs and know the importance of relationship as per consumers' perception, have greater chances to sustain in the relationship.

When a financial organization is framing its strategic intent and fixing the KPIs for customer-related parameters in case they put commitment

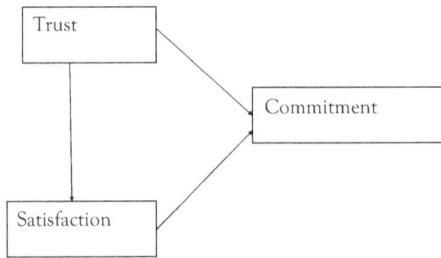

Figure 5.1 The relationship between "satisfaction," "trust," and "commitment"

as an objective, it becomes logical and important to design its programs, systems, and policies in a manner that automatically take care of satisfaction and trust. This would again be unique to the financial organization and a factor to differentiate from its competitors. The competitive state of the financial organization will help fix the customer-related objective between/or acquisition and retention. All this would fall under the purview of the management of the financial organization and thus management commitment would be an important variable for the successful implementation of a customer-oriented service plan. For enforcement since operations are the backbone of such an organization as highlighted in Chapters 3 and 4, technology would be a key resource. At the end, the most important fact for a financial organization is to value the customer and understand his expectations and accordingly plan the delivery on those expectations.

Conclusion

This chapter establishes the relationship between the constructs of "satisfaction," "trust," and "commitment." The key takeaways from this chapter are:

i. An implementation framework for marketing strategy based on customer orientation.
ii. Establish the importance satisfaction, trust, and commitment for relationship building.
iii. Each financial organization must have a unique marketing strategy.

References

Ahmad Abuarqoub, I. 2019. "Language Barriers to Effective Communication." *Utopía y Praxis Latinoamericana* 24.

Akerlof, G.A. and R.E. Kranton. 2005. "Identity and the Economics of Organizations." *Journal of Economic perspectives* 19, no. 1, pp. 9–32.

Alley, T.R. and J.A. Schutheis. 2001. "Is Facial Skin Tone Sufficient to Produce a Cross-Racial Identification Effect?" *Perceptual and Motor Skills* 92, pp. 1191–1198.

Allmér, H. 2014. "E-Servicescape Is Plausible."

American Marketing Association. 2017. www.ama.org/the-definition-of-marketing-what-is-marketing/.

Bagozzi, R.P. 1975. "Social Exchange in Marketing." *Journal of the Academy of Marketing Science* 3, no. 3, pp. 314–327.

Beamer, L. 1992. "Learning Intercultural Communication Competence." *The Journal of Business Communication* 29, pp. 285–303.

Bitner, M.J. 1992. "Servicescapes: The Impact of Physical Surroundings on Customers and Employees." *Journal of Marketing* 56, no. 2, pp. 57–71.

Boli, J. and M.A. Elliott. 2008. "Facade Diversity: The Individualization of Cultural Difference." *International Sociology* 23, no. 540–560.

Caldwell, D.F. and C.A. O'Reilly, III. 1990. "Measuring Person-Job Fit With a Profile-Comparison Process." *Journal of Applied Psychology* 75, no. 6, p. 648.

Chaney, L.H. and J.S. Martin. 2000. *Intercultural Business Communication.* Upper Saddle River, NJ: Prentice Hall.

Czepiel, J.A., M.R. Solomon, C.F. Surprenant, and E.G. Gutman. 1985. "Service Encounters: An Overview." In *The Service Encounter: Managing Employee/ Customer Interaction in Service Businesses*, eds., J.A. Czepiel, M.R. Solomon, and C.F. Surprenant, pp. 3–15. Lexington, MA: Lexington Books.

Dahl, S. 1998. *Communications and Culture Transformation: Cultural Diversity, Globalization and Cultural Convergence.* Project presented to the European University, Barcelona. UK: University of Luton.

Dailey, L. 2004. "Navigational Web Atmospherics: Explaining the Influence of Restrictive Navigation Cues." *Journal of Business Research* 57, no. 7, pp. 795–803.

Darby, M.R. and E. Karni. April 1973. "Free Competition and the Optimal Amount of Fraud." *Journal of Law and Economics* 16, pp. 67–88.

Ferguson, D.P., G. Rhodes, and K. Lee. 2001. "They All Look Alike to Me: Prejudice and Cross-Face Recognition." *British Journal of Psychology* 92, pp. 567–577.

Fernandez, A., D. Schillinger, K. Grumbach, A. Rosenthal, A.L. Stewart, F. Wang, and E.J. Pérez-Stable. 2004. "Physician Language Ability and Cultural Competence." *Journal of general internal medicine* 19, no. 2, pp. 167–174.

Ferraro, P.J. and R.G. Cummings. 2007. "Cultural Diversity, Discrimination, and Economic Outcomes: An Experimental Analysis." *Economic Inquiry* 45, pp. 217–232.

Fisher, C., D. Doughty, and S. Mussayeva. 2008. "Learning and Tensions in Managerial Intercultural Encounters: A Dialectical Interpretation." *Management Learning* 39, pp. 311–327.

Fitzsimmons, J.A. and M.J. Fitzsimmons. 2003. *Service Management: Operations, Strategy, and Information Technology*. Boston: McGraw-Hill.

Grönroos, C. 1984. "A Service Quality Model and Its Marketing Implications." *European Journal of marketing*.

Grove, S.J. and R.P. Fisk. 1992. "The Service Experience as Theater." *ACR North American Advances* 19, eds., J.F. Sherry, Jr. and B. Sternthal, Provo, UT: Association for Consumer Research, pp. 455–461.

Gutek, B.A., B. Cherry, A.D. Bhappu, S. Schneider, and L. Woolf. 2000. "Features of Service Relationships and Encounters." *Work and occupations* 27, no. 3, pp. 319–352.

Harris, L.C. and C. Ezeh. 2008. "Servicescape and Loyalty Intentions: An Empirical Investigation." *European Journal of Marketing*.

Harris, L.C. and M.M. Goode. 2010. "Online Servicescapes, Trust, and Purchase Intentions." *Journal of Services Marketing*.

Heskett, J.L., T.O. Jones, G.W. Loveman, W.E. Sasser, and L.A. Schlesinger. 1994. "Putting the Service-Profit Chain to Work." *Harvard Business Review* 72, no. 2, pp. 164–174.

Hoffman, B.J. and D.J. Woehr. 2006. "A Quantitative Review of the Relationship Between Person–Organization Fit and Behavioral Outcomes." *Journal of Vocational Behavior* 68, no. 3, pp. 389–399.

Hogg, M.A. and D.J. Terry. 2000. "Social Identity and Self-Categorization Processes in Organizational Contexts." *Academy of Management Review* 25, pp. 121–140.

Holbrook, M.B. 1999. "Consumer Value." *A Framework for Analysis and Research*. London: Routledge.

Hopkins, W.E. and S.A. Hopkins. 2002. "Effects of Cultural Recomposition on Group Interaction Processes." *Academy of Management Review* 27, pp. 541–553.

Hopkins, S.A., W. Nie, and W.E. Hopkins. 2009. "Cultural Effects on Customer Satisfaction With Service Encounters." *Journal of Service Science (JSS)* 2, no. 1, pp. 45–56.

Jones, E., J.N. Moore, A.J.S. Stanaland, and R.A.J. Wyatt. 1998. "Salesperson Race and Gender and the Access and Legitimacy Paradigm: Does Difference Make a Difference?" *Journal of Personal Selling and Sales Management* 18, pp. 71–88.

Kristof-Brown, A.L., R.D. Zimmerman, and E.C. Johnson. 2005. "Consequences of Individuals' Fit at work: A Meta-Analysis of person–Job, Person–Organization, Person–Group, and Person–Supervisor Fit." *Personnel Psychology* 58, no. 2, pp. 281–342.

Lai, K.P., S.C. Chong, H.B. Ismail, and D.Y.K. Tong. 2014. "An Explorative Study of Shopper-Based Salient E-Servicescape Attributes: A Means-End Chain Approach." *International Journal of Information Management* 34, no. 4, pp. 517–532.

Lauver, K.J. and A. Kristof-Brown. 2001. "Distinguishing Between Employees' Perceptions of Person–Job and Person–Organization Fit." *Journal of Vocational Behavior* 59, no. 3, pp. 454–470.

Levin, D.T. 2000. "Race as a Visual Feature: Using Visual Search and Perceptual Discrimination Tasks to Understand Face Categories and the Cross-Race Recognition Deficit." *Journal of Experimental Psychology* 129, pp. 559–574.

Lovelock, C.H. 1994. *Product Plus: How Product + Service = Competitive Advantage*. New York, NY: McGraw-Hill.

Lovelock, C.H. 1996. "Adding Value to Core Products With Supplementary Services." In *Service Services Marketing*, 2nd ed., pp. 337–359. NJ: Prentice Hall.

Maister, D.H. 1984. *The Psychology of Waiting Lines*. Boston: Harvard Business School.

Mattila, A.S. 1999. "The Role of Culture in the Service Evaluation Process." *Journal of Service Research* 1, pp. 250–261.

Milliken, F.J. and L.L. Martins. 1996. "Searching for Common Threads: Understanding the Multiple Effects of Diversity in Organizational Groups." *Academy of Management Review* 21, pp. 402–433.

Mishkin. 2007. *The Economics of Money, Banking and Financial Markets*, Addison Wesley, 8th ed., p. 24.

Moorman, C., G. Zaltman, and R. Deshpande. 1992. "Relationships Between Providers and Users of Market Research: The Dynamics of Trust Within and Between Organizations." *Journal of Marketing Research* 29, no. 3, pp. 314–328.

Morgan, R.M. and S.D. Hunt. 1994. "The Commitment-Trust Theory of Relationship Marketing." *Journal of Marketing* 58, no. 3, pp. 20–38.

Muchinsky, P.M. and C.J. Monahan. 1987. "What Is Person-Environment Congruence? Supplementary Versus Complementary Models of Fit." *Journal of Vocational Behavior* 31, no. 3, pp. 268–277.

Nelson, P. 1974. "Advertising as Information." *Journal of Political Economy* 82, no. 4, pp. 729–754. www.jstor.org/stable/1837143.

Oliver, R.L. 2006. "Customer Satisfaction Research." *The Handbook of Marketing Research: Uses, Misuses, and Future Advances* 1.

Papadopoulou, P., P. Kanellis, and D. Martakos. 2002. "Trust Formation and Relationship Building in Electronic Servicescapes." In *ECIS*, pp. 1487–1497.

Parasuraman, A., V.A. Zeithaml, and L.L. Berry. 1985. "A Conceptual Model of Service Quality and Its Implications for Future Research." *Journal of Marketing* 49, no. 4, pp. 41–50.

Rusbult, C.E. 1980. "Commitment and Satisfaction in Romantic Associations: A Test of the Investment Model." *Journal of experimental social psychology* 16, no. 2, pp. 172–186.

Rusbult, C.E. and D. Farrell. 1983. "A Longitudinal Test of the Investment Model: The Impact on Job Satisfaction, Job Commitment, and Turnover of Variations in Rewards, Costs, Alternatives, and Investments." *Journal of Applied Psychology* 68, no. 3, pp. 429–438.

Schneider, B. and D.E. Bowen. 1985. "Employee and Customer Perceptions of Service in Banks: Replication and Extension." *Journal of Applied Psychology* 70, no. 3, p. 423.

Shostack, L. 1985. "Planning the Service Encounter." In *The Service Encounter: Managing Employee/Customer Interaction in Service Businesses*, eds., J.A. Czepiel, M.R. Solomon, and C.F. Surprenant, pp. 243–254. Lexington, MA: Lexington Books.

Sporer, S.L. 2001. "Eyewitness Identification: Recognizing Faces of Other Ethnic Groups: And Integration of Theories." *Psychology, Public Policy and Law* 7, pp. 1–45.

Sreejesh, S. and P. Abhilash. 2017. "Investigating the Process Through Which E-Servicescape Creates E-Loyalty in Travel and Tourism Websites." *Journal of Travel and Tourism Marketing* 34, no. 1, pp. 20–39.

Srivastava. R. 2004. *Evaluation of Relationship Marketing in the Financial Services Sector: An Indian Perspective* (Unpublished doctoral dissertation). Lucknow: University of Lucknow.

Stauss, B. and P. Mang. 1999. "'Culture Shocks' in Inter-Cultural Service Encounters." *Journal of Services Marketing* 13, no. 4/5, pp. 329–346.

Stewart, D.M. and E.C. Jackson. 2003. "Matching Customer Scripts and Service Encounter Designs." *Proceedings of the Decision Sciences Institute National Conference*.

Sulman, J., M. Kanee, and D. Savage. 2007. "Does Difference Matter? Diversity and Human Rights in a Hospital Workplace." *The Journal of Health Care Social Work* 44, pp. 145–159.

Surprenant, C.F. and M.R. Solomon. 1987. "Predictability and Personalization in the Service Encounter." *Journal of Marketing* 51, pp. 86–96.

Tajfel, H. and J.C. Turner. 1979. "An Integrative Theory of Intergroup Conflict." In *The Social Psychology of Intergroup Relations*, eds., W.G. Austin and S. Worchel, pp. 33–47. Monterey, CA: Brooks-Cole.

Turner, J.C., M.A. Hogg, P.J. Oakes, S.D. Reicher, and M. Wetherell. 1987. *Rediscovering the Social Group: A Self-Categorization Theory*. Oxford, England: Basil Blackwell.

Zeithaml, V.A., L.L. Berry, and A. Parasuraman. 1993. "The Nature and Determinants of Customer Expectations of Service." *Journal of the Academy of Marketing Science* 21, no. 1, pp. 1–12.

Zeithaml, V.A. and M.J. Bitner. 2000. *Services Marketing: Integrating Customer Focus Across the Firm*, 2nd Edition. Boston: McGraw-Hill.

APPENDIX 1

Financial Goals Worksheet

Date

Goal	Target date to achieve goal	Priority A = Critical B = Need C = Want	Current savings toward goal	Additional savings needed per week or month
Goals for the short term (6 months to 5 years)				
Mid-term objectives 5 to 10 years				
Long-term objectives (greater than 10 years)				

Source: https://secure02.principal.com/publicvsupply/GetFile?fm=MD1433A&ty=VOP&EXT=. VOP

Customer Service Sample Voice Prompts for Banks and Related Financial Services

Introduction

This document contains illustrative samples of scripts for professionally recorded voice prompts for banking and associated financial services enterprises, ranging from large, national/international corporations to small- and medium-sized local community banks. They're designed to generate ideas for companies that wish to improve customer service through a well-thought-out voice–user interface, and they may be tailored to the company's unique services and organizational structure.

Table of Contents

Traditionally, most banks have simply provided rudimentary greetings and call distribution prompts, leaving them behind in terms of customer care. By expanding their prompts to automate banking procedures such as location information, opening hours, rates, and disclosures, these firms can improve their capacity to route clients to the appropriate goods and services. Here is a list of several types of banking prompts to give you an idea of what you can do for a more inclusive approach—each with examples. The descriptions and sample scripts for each situation are listed in the following sections.

1. Greeting and Call Distribution

Generic Banking Services

For a local bank or credit union, a typical auto attendant greeting and call distribution tree can be reviewed for several specialty departments or functions, key resources, and ways to access various banking or information services.

> Thank you for getting in touch with XYZ Bank.
> To get help with Internet or mobile banking, dial 1.
> To sign up for a new Internet or mobile banking service, dial 2.
> For questions about debit or credit cards, dial 3.
> For questions about loans and mortgages, dial 4.
> Press 5 or stay on the line for an operator for assistance with additional services.

Multilingual Greeting

It's critical to cater to a broad customer base. An example of a bilingual greeting prompt is listed as follows.

> Thank you for getting in touch with XYZ Bank.
> To get help with Internet or mobile banking, press 1.
> To sign up for a new online or mobile banking service, press 1, 2.
> Or, in the case of all other goods and services, press 3.

(Followed by a Spanish version) Para recibir asistencia con la banca móvil o en línea, oprima 1. Para inscribirse en un nuevo servicio de banca móvil o en línea, oprima 2. O, para todos los otros productos o servicios, oprima 3.

Note: Your phone tech or programmer can create a phone tree with an introductory welcome that directs the caller to prompts in their preferred language.

Example:

Press 1 to continue in English.
Mark number 2 for Espanol.

Specific Departments

Special departments and operatives are required by banks and financial service businesses to deal with specific demands for information, such as loans, mortgages, and routine customer care questions. Consider the following example:

To get help with Internet or mobile banking, dial 1.
To sign up for a new Internet or mobile banking service, dial 2.
Press 3 for additional XYZ Bank products and services.

This menu's response directs the caller to a more particular department or person, as follows:

Press 1 to check the status of your loan application.
Press 2 to apply for a loan or line of credit.
Press 3 to apply for a credit card.
Press 4 if you have any queries regarding switching your existing Home Equity lines to a fixed rate.
Press 5 to learn more about other products and services.
Please press 6 for existing account information.

Busy/On Hold

We value the time you spend on the phone with us. All of our customer service representatives are now assisting other customers; please wait for the next available agent. For further information and commonly asked questions, please visit our e-branch upgrading page at X Y Z Bank dot com.

2. Bank Access

Location, Directions, and Hours of Operation

Typical banks have many sites where they have branches. With a well-designed auto attendant system leading consumers to the correct locations at the right times—and referring the caller to a web-based map or directions resource—finding a bank branch, an ATM, or a drive-up window facility may be quick and easy.

Press 1 for places in the Central Valley. Press 2 for destinations in the East Valley and 3 for locations in the North Valley. Press 4 for places in the South Valley and 5 for locations in the West Valley.

If number "3" was pressed, it would be followed by

The following is a list of XYZ locations in the South Valley, including 16th Street and Collins. Our 16th Street location is located at 2323 East Southern Avenue in Phoenix. Monday through Friday, 9:00 a.m. to 6:00 p.m., and Saturday, 9:00 a.m. to 1:00 p.m. Holiday closures are not included in the listed hours; 54321 South 47th Street, just south of Chandler Boulevard, is where our Collins branch is located. Monday through Friday, 9 a.m. to 6 p.m., are the regular hours. On Saturdays, the Collins branch is closed.

Branch Addresses (Speech Recognition)

Customers are frequently given the option of choosing from a list of various walk-in or ATM service locations and being directed to one of them. An IVR application can route a client call depending on the service sought, as well as offer location information, using speech recognition and audio prompts.

Initial Location Menu

Say "West" or press 1 for Western Idaho, and "East" or press 2 for Eastern Idaho. Say "Central" or push 3 for Central Idaho. Say "North" or press 4 to reach Northern Idaho. Say "Go back" or hit star to return to the previous menu.

Postlocation Menu

Say "Repeat That" or press 1 to hear this location information again. Say "go back" or press 2 to return to the list of destinations. Say "new search" or press star to start a new branch or ATM search. Say "Main Menu" or press 9 for help with something else. Otherwise, if you're finished, you may disconnect.

Switchboard Closed

Our switchboard is currently closed, thank you for calling XYZ Federal Bank. Our phone lines are open from 9 a.m. to 6 p.m. Monday through Friday, and Saturday from 9 a.m. to 1 p.m. You can contact immediately 866-555-5432 to report your Visa card as lost or stolen. Please hit pound if you'd like to be sent to our Visa hotline.

Holiday Closure

Thank you for getting in touch with XYZ Bank. Owing to the holiday season, we will be closed during this time.

You can input the extension number of the person you're attempting to reach at any moment, or press 9 for an Employee Directory if you know it.

Press 1 for home loans, 2 for business loans, and 3 for ATM locations.
Press 4 to report a lost or stolen credit or ATM card.
Press 5 to leave a message in our general mailbox and receive a callback the next working day.

3. Information/Disclosure

Outbound Informational Calls

An informational call is intended to provide you with information about your account. Informational calls could cover topics like [pause] suspected fraudulent behavior on your account, [pause] notifying you that you have missed a loan payment, or [pause] telling you of other signif-icant changes to your account. Telemarketing calls are not the same as informational calls. If you have not opted out, ABC may call the mobile phone numbers you have provided to us for informational purposes uti-lizing an automatic telephone dialing system. An automatic telephone dialing system is a piece of software that can [pause] store and generate random or sequential phone numbers, as well as [pause] dial them.

Example:

ABC Bank may contact you via an automated telephone dialing sys-tem to discuss your account on a regular basis; leave you a voice, prere-corded, or artificial voice message; or send you a message, e-mail, or other electronic message to service your account, collect any amounts you may owe, or for any other informational purposes related to your account at any number you have provided us. When using an automated telephone dialing system, you have the option of opting out of informational rea-sons. ABC's right to call you in any manner allowed by law will not be affected by your directive. You do not need to do anything if you have previously decided to opt out of ABC making informational calls to your cell phone via an automated telephone calling system.

Interest Rates

Regularly updating and sharing interest rates, fees, annual percentage rate (APR), and other information is a wonderful method to keep clients informed as part of the timely tree.

For the XYZ Credit Card, we must provide you with the following important rate, fee, and other cost information. The APR for purchases on XYZ credit card accounts range from 13.99 to 24.99 percent, depend-ing on your credit worthiness. Balance transfers and cash advances have a 25.99 percent APR. Based on the prime rate, all APRs will fluctuate with the market.

If interest is applied, the fee will be no less than $2.00. There isn't a yearly fee. This cost information is up-to-date as of today.

Residents of New York can acquire a comparison of credit card rates, fees, and grace periods from the New York State Department of Financial

Services. New York State Department of Financial Services can be reached at 1(800)518-8866 or at www.dfs.ny.gov.

Credit Report Disclosure/Consent

Credit reports may be ordered in connection with the processing of applications/solicitations, as well as any updates, renewals, or extensions of credit. We will provide you with the name and address of any consumer reporting agency that provided a report on you if requested. By signing or otherwise submitting an application or proposal, you authorize the procurement of such reports.

State Legal Disclosure

Residents of Wisconsin: No provision of a marital property agreement, unilateral statement under Section 766.59, or court decree under Section 766.70 adversely affects ABC Bank's interest unless the bank receives a copy of the agreement, statement, or decree prior to the time credit is granted, or has actual knowledge of the adverse provision when the obligation to the bank is incurred. Thank you for taking the time to listen. Please press 1 right now if you'd like to learn more about the XYZ prepaid MasterCard.

Residents of Ohio: Under Ohio's antidiscrimination legislation, all creditors must make credit equally available to all creditworthy consumers, and credit reporting companies must retain separate credit histories on each individual upon request. Compliance with this law is overseen by the Ohio Civil Rights Commission.

Adapted from www.marketingmessages.com

APPENDIX 3

When Serving Customers Became Tough?

We live in a fast-paced, technologically evolved, globally interconnected society teeming with people, technology, organizations, and their diverse competing interests. A basic task like looking for a plumber to fix a leaky basin can lead to a maze of channels, views, promoters, and behind-the-scenes mechanisms. Everyone influences a customer's cognition and behavior, from Google to Yelp to Aunt Polly. As a result, customer service has become more difficult than it has ever been. The key differentiator between a successful and unsuccessful firm is service. Customers expect better, more personalized service from the moment they walk into a store or place an order. It entails being available 24 hours a day, seven days a week, and ready to be professional, convivial, and receptive at all times. This is especially critical for small firms that rely on excellent customer service to outperform larger competitors.

With all of this in mind, many business owners become perplexed while trying to figure out the customer service equation:

- Which services should I spend my money on?
- What are the most important qualities in a customer service representative?
- What matters most to your customers?

It doesn't have to be difficult. It is not necessary to compromise on quality or to be available to clients at all times. Regardless of size or industry, a company can provide excellent customer service in-house, through outsourcing, or through a combination of the two: online or in person.

Checklist for Customer Service Audits

Begin with the fundamentals.

Before you start worrying about more advanced customer experience protocols, be sure your company has a solid foundation that allows you to deliver on your promises.

1. A powerful and adaptable customer service infrastructure.
   Serving consumers according to their availability and accessibility is a crucial aspect of running a business. Customers want businesses to be available in a variety of ways, including in person, over the phone, in the mail, on the Web, and on social media, so they may contact them whenever and however they want. Certain types of consumer services must be offered at all times of the year, without exception. Customers do not always adhere to business hours, especially when there are product or service issues. For many firms, managing internally is not feasible or cost-effective; in these circumstances, on-demand virtual receptionist services come in handy.

2. A customer service crew that has been thoroughly trained.
   The frontline workers must be well-prepared and knowledgeable in advance. Furthermore, the employees must be well-trained in greeting, welcoming, dealing with difficult situations, and so on.

3. Continuing education in customer service is a continuous activity.
   Training is a long-term commitment. Members of the customer service staff should be updated and trained on a regular basis through refresher and other short-term training exercises, with a focus on continuous education and improvement.

4. Customer help over the phone is available.
   It is critical to have a business phone line that is answered by a live person as often as possible. Voicemail and/or interactive voice response (IVR) systems are disliked by customers. Every missed call is an opportunity missed.

5. Obtaining easily accessible phone number.
   To avoid misunderstanding, a business phone number should be easily accessible and limited in number. The phone number for the

company should be visible on the website, social media, and other locations. The statistics should be easily visible in a web search.

6. Customer help via live chat is available.

Chat is preferred by 42 percent of all customers over other contact channels, and 73 percent of customers reported satisfaction. Chat may convert prospects into customers 4.6 times faster than other channels.

7. Customer help via e-mail is available.

Because not all clients want to converse, firms must be prepared to receive and respond to e-mails. Inboxes should be examined at least once a day and responses should be returned within 24 hours. E-mail addresses, like phone numbers, must be freely accessible.

8. Customer help is available via social media.

Customers are increasingly using social media to connect with brands. Failure to respond to their comments and messages may cause such customers to defect to your competitors. A social media plan should be incorporated in any customer care program, regardless of the company's size, location, or industry.

9. A pleasant social atmosphere—physically, digitally, or both.

The most overlooked part of the customer service experience is the consumer's first encounter with the business environment. Lobbies, offices, and waiting rooms are examples of physical business places, as are websites and other digital spaces. Basic questions to consider in physical spaces include the following:

- When customers walk inside your establishment, how do they feel?
- What do you think the first thing they notice is?
- Is there a location to sit that is both pleasant and convenient?
- As soon as a customer walks through the front door, they should feel welcomed and enticed.
- A website must be quick to load, easy to navigate, and compatible with all devices. Customers can use all of the information they need about a company before contacting them to make decisions and take action, such as making a purchase or signing up for a mailing list.

10. You have off-hours and after-hours service support.

Customer assistance must be available at all times. When clients wish to contact the company outside of typical working hours or when it's busy, there should be a solution. Outsourcing could be a viable option.

11. There are no long lines for customer assistance.

Customers despise having to wait for when and how to contact them. Around 80 percent of clients expect assistance within an hour of contacting you, and about 75 percent expect service within five minutes. The longer a customer waits, the more likely they are to switch to a competition.

12. Calls are efficiently checked and transferred.

Customer service excellence begins even before a company picks up a customer's phone call. When a business is busy, it can divert calls to the appropriate individual or to another representative. People can be trained to attend and transfer calls in the absence of automated systems, by requesting information and responding appropriately.

13. Team members greet visitors in a professional and friendly manner.

Both correct and inappropriate greetings are acceptable. "Hello," "Thank you for calling," "Good morning/afternoon," or a combination of the three can be used. Give the name of the company. Telling callers more than "Hello" can be confusing; give them more so they know they've dialed the correct number.

Make an effort to assist. Instead of dealing with questions directly, ask "How may I help you?" or "How may I assist you?" and when transferring calls, "How may I direct your call?" If you have a query, such as "What is your account number?" or "May I have your account number, please?" you can ask it now in a professional and kind manner.

14. Offer client care in a variety of languages.

For enterprises, being completely monolingual is not a viable choice. Providing services in several languages of comparable quality to each individual can be beneficial to a business, and a company should learn how to deal with language barriers.

15. Team members engage in active listening exercises.

Customers are the focus of customer service. Being truly present in customer encounters demonstrates that you care about them.

That entails paying close attention to what a consumer wants or needs and never presuming what they want or need. Taking notes, offering tiny verbal clues ("yeah," "that's right," and "mm-hmm"), repeating what is heard, and responding in ways that reflect attentiveness are all strategies to practice active listening. Active listening is a skill that can be mastered with practice and patience.

16. Team members' product and/or service knowledge.

Customer service professionals must be knowledgeable about the products and services that their company offers. They should not have as much information as a salesperson, but they should have the fundamentals and demonstrate some competence in the sector or niche—the challenges, concerns, terminology, technology, updates, and trends that are unique to a business.

17. Team members maintain a cheerful, personal, and quick tone in their talks.

Customer service should be centered on the customer. Customers don't want to waste time in meaningless conversation, and prefer to be handled in a pleasant or personable manner. Answering as quickly as possible, greeting courteously, customization, professionalism, and tranquilly are all ways that customer service workers can achieve the right balance. It's important to pay equal attention to avoiding unnecessary hitches, avoiding cul-de-sacs, and not dwelling on mistakes.

18. Team members are aware of and follow all applicable rules and regulations.

Customer support representatives should receive training on rules and regulations that are relevant to the company. It entails not only following the rules and avoiding fines and prison time but also treating consumers ethically and respectfully. The behavior of the customer care team members reflects the business's behavior, which is why adequate training is necessary.

19. Team members express brand principles in a clear and concise manner.

When team members communicate, they should do so in a way that reflects the brand. The objective, purpose, and values of the firm should be reflected in the customer service staff. Customers should feel a sense of exclusivity or a distinguishing quality about a company when they contact a representative.

Make things happen.

By contacting individuals frequently, you might become a firm that people admire. Customize interactions go above and above, and take interaction to the next level to provide customers an experience.

20. Make service interactions more personalized.

Building and nurturing connections should be prioritized in order to win clients' trust. Customers become loyal followers and brand advocates when they see the company as a valuable resource or a friend, rather than merely a service provider. Here are a few relationship-building strategies:

Every customer's name should be remembered and used.

Send communications that aren't (explicitly) "salesy," such as birthday or anniversary cards.

As a service, provide each consumer what they require.

21. Team members who are effective in handling queries.

Using the phrase "I don't know" can be detrimental to a company's bottom line. It is not necessary to know everything, but it is necessary to know how to deal with uncertainty. It is preferable to find solutions to satisfy their request as best as a team can, by requesting time or providing alternatives.

22. Assist team members in resolving client complaints and providing better service.

Giving frontline customer service representatives the authority and control they desire may enable them to provide better service. Customers would be thrilled as well, as this empowerment would make staff feel appreciated, significant, and treasured.

23. When necessary, customer enquiries and issues are escalated.

When the customer care team is unable to assist someone, a backup channel or process should be available to handle or serve the situation. In addition, if a customer has a problem with a customer care person, he or she should have the information and resources to file a complaint and discuss the matter with a supervisor.

24. Team members should be aware of the needs of clients ahead of time.

A strong customer care team should be aware of the types of needs that a customer might have. It could be accomplished by reading clues and performing little behaviors. Send a product or a note to a client who was unable to attend a meeting due to unforeseen circumstances.

25. Team members cultivate customer relationships.

    Excellent customer service requires a strong sense of connection. It's a cost-effective strategy to grow your audience and revenue. Making meaningful connections aids in the development of relationships and the provision of excellent service.

26. After an interaction with a consumer, members of the team follow up with them.

    When a call or an online chat with a customer finishes, it's important to keep the conversation going by sending a thank-you note by e-mail or text, along with any relevant information or discount offers, to demonstrate concern and care.

27. At work, team members are engaged and joyful.

    It is critical for customer service professionals to be happy in order to make consumers happy. According to studies, there is a strong link between employee engagement and consumer satisfaction.

28. Create a healthy, inclusive workplace atmosphere.

    Employee engagement and culture are inextricably linked, and both are beneficial to business success. Healthy corporate cultures develop where people feel comfortable, are willing to be vulnerable, and share a purpose, according to Daniel Coyle, author of *The Culture Code: The Secrets of Highly Successful Groups*. The organizational culture should be diverse and inclusive; when people leave, they take their ideas, perspectives, and personalities with them. Together, they build a powerful community. Encourage employees to collaborate, support one another, share in one other's triumphs, and donate to something bigger than themselves in order to establish and foster culture.

29. You've set customer service KPIs and are tracking them.

    It is difficult to attain or measure goals without defining them. That is, connecting customer service initiatives to larger corporate objectives will help it improve. Key performance indicators (KPIs) should be stated, monitored, and measured by businesses. Customer satisfaction (CSAT) score, customer effort score (CES), net promoter score (NPS), churn rate, response time, retention rate, and resolution time are all common customer service indicators.

30. Keep track of existing and potential clients' transactions.

    Customers should not be asked for information that has already been disclosed to them by customer support representatives. Customers find it aggravating. It's a good idea to keep note of who's contacting you, when they're contacting you, and why. There are numerous customer relationship management (CRM) software available; investigate your alternatives and, if necessary, create a system for your company.

31. Go beyond transactional engagements to get feedback from customers. Customers should be asked for feedback on how to improve their experiences, which should not be restricted to product reviews and/or business ratings. Know who your consumers are and how you can best serve them. Likes, interests, dislikes, and suggestions should all be taken into account.

32. Your customer service strategy and company model integrate feedback.

    Rather than listening, action should be taken in response to what customers say. Show that you care about your customers by tailoring items and services to their specific requirements. It is meaningless to supply services if clients dislike them.

About the Author

Prof. Ritu Srivastava is an academician by heart, with a firm belief that management education goes beyond classroom and includes various components on industry interaction, social outreach, and research and development. The core of Dr. Srivastava's work centers around the industry with the firm belief that management education at all levels has to be absorbed by the industry. Her research ideas have been appreciated at national and international marketing conferences. She is also the Chair of CII Indian Women Network, Haryana Chapter.

Dr. Srivastava has been offering courses on Marketing Implementation, Campaign Management, Services Marketing, Relationship Marketing, Marketing Insights, Retailing and Franchising, and Integrated Marketing Communication including digital platforms. She received the award for "Teaching Excellence" at MDI, Gurgaon, for the year 2019 to 2020.

In the recent past, Dr. Srivastava has conducted several training programs for various public sector enterprises and private firms like BEL, MES, DGET, DST, DGET, LIC, NADP, Canon India, and Vodafone. She also has developed a simulation, "Customer Black Box," which is being used by B-schools for Marketing Management. She has been spearheading faculty development programs for other B-school faculty in India, with the idea of developing a teaching learning community that brings quality to the management classrooms and is also able to handle India-specific managerial issues.

Dr. Srivastava's research interest lies in the area of service marketing, service quality, customer experience management, low-income customers, and emerging markets. Her text book on *Retailing Management* by Pearson is a bestseller. She also has a research reference book on low customers in India published by Business Expert Press. An avid case writer, she has published with leading publishers such as Richard Ivey School of Business, Emerald Emerging Market Case Studies, and Sage Business Cases, apart from scholarly research published in high-impact journals.

Dr. Srivastava has a rich consultancy experience of 26 projects in both government and private sectors.

Index

Accidental loss, 6
Affordable premium, 6
Agency functions, 4–5
Assets assessment, 25
Assurance, 86

Banking institutions, 2
Blueprinting, 55–58
Bond funds, 13

Calculable loss, 6
Capital market, 2
Catastrophically large losses, 7
Commercial banks, 3–5
Commitment, 101–102
Consumer decision making, 42
    postpurchase evaluation, 43
    prepurchase, 40–41
    purchase, 41–43
Cooperatives, 12
Corporate stocks, 13
Cultural identification strength, 54
Culture, 51–55
Culture differences, 52–53
Customer-centric approach, 88
Customer expectations, 83–85
    adequate level, 60–61
    desired level, 60–61
    exceeding, 72–73
    framework, 62
    management, 67–68
        integrated marketing
            communication, 73–78
        Psychology of Waiting Lines,
            68–72
        ways of influencing, 67–68
    in marketing financial products,
        59–66
    market research, 91–93
Customer misbehavior, 46–47
    dealing, 48–51
    effects of, 47–48
    reasons, 47

Customer-oriented implementation
        plan
    for financial organizations, 99–102
Customer perceptions, 83–85, 87,
        91–93
Customer satisfaction, 101–102
    in every service interaction, 88
    expectations, 83–85
    giving evidence of service, 87–88
    managing service employees for,
        93–96
    measurements, 88
    organizing service employees, 96–98
    perceptions, 83–85, 87
    quality of service, 88
    service quality dimensions, 85–87

Definite loss, 6

Emotions and moods, 41, 43
Empathy, 86–87
E-servicescape, 81

Fiduciary responsibility, 2
Financial goals, 21–24
Financial institutions, 2–5
Financial product experience
        designing, 44–45
    culture, 51–55
    customer misbehavior, 46–47
        dealing, 48–51
        effects of, 47–48
        reasons, 47
    service scripts, 45

Gaps model, 84, 85, 88–91, 98

Income, 17, 20–21
Indemnification policy, 8
Indemnify, 8–9
Individual financial planning, 16–17
    areas, 17
    example, 24–26

financial goals, 21–24
income, 17
income evaluation, 20–21
investing, 19
money management, 20–21
monitoring, 26–27
protection, 20
reassessment, 26–27
saving, 18–19
spending, 17–18
Information search, 40
Insurance
    companies, 3–5
    indemnification concept, 8–9
    legal requirements, 7
    services, 6
    social effects, 9–10
Intangibility, 34–35
Integrated marketing communication,
    73–78
Internal marketing communication
    management, 77–78
Investment, 19

JAYCustomers, 46–50

Large loss, 6

Money management, 20–21
Money market, 2
Money market funds, 13
Money psychology, 15–16
Mutual funds
    benefits, 12–14
    buying and selling, 14–15
    risks, 13–14
    types, 13

Nonbanking financial institution
    (NBFI), 10
    facilitate growth, 11
    in financial system, 10–11
    promote stability, 11–12

Pay on behalf, 8
Pension fund, 12, 15
Personal financial plan, 24
    assets assessment, 25
    insurance coverage, 25

joint expenses, 26
retirement expenses, 25–26
Personal financial protection, 20
Personality traits theory, 95
Person–Organization fit (P–O fit), 95
Positioning strategy, 28–29
Provider gaps, 84–85, 88–91
Psychology of Waiting Lines, 68–72

Quality of service, 88

Reimbursement policy, 8
Reliability, 86
Reserve Bank of India (RBI), 4
Responsiveness, 87
Retail financial products, 1–2
    classification, 37–40
    commercial banks, 3–5
    cooperatives, 12
    fiduciary responsibility, 2
    financial institutions, 2, 3–5
    financial markets, 2
    financial services
        characteristics, 33–37
        heterogeneity, 35–36
        intangibility, 34–35
        perishability, 36–37
        simultaneous production and
            consumption, 36
    financial system, 3
        characteristic features, 1–2
        nonbanking financial institution
            (NBFI) in, 10–11
    insurance
        companies, 3–5
        indemnification concept, 8–9
        legal requirements, 7
        social effects, 9–10
    marketing, 27–29
    mutual funds
        benefits, 12–14
        buying and selling, 14–15
        risks, 13–14
        types, 13
    nonbanking financial institution
        (NBFI), 10
        facilitate growth, 11
        in financial system, 10–11
        promote stability, 11–12

pension fund, 12, 15
service concept, 30–31

Saving, 18–19
Service concept, 30–31
Service interaction, 88
Service marketing, 29
Service operations, 29
Servicescape, 78–82
Service scripts, 45, 51
Services marketing system, 55–58
SERVQUAL scale, 86–87, 98
Socialization, 79

Specific, measurable, achievable,
    relevant, and timely (SMART)
    goals, 24
Spending, 17–18
Strategic marketing planning, 27, 28
Superannuation fund. *See* Pension
    funds

Tangibles, 86
Target date funds, 13
Trust, 101–102

Ways of influencing, 67–68

OTHER TITLES IN THE MARKETING COLLECTION

Naresh Malhotra, Georgia Tech, Editor

- *The Big Miss* by Zhecho Dobrev
- *Digital Brand Romance* by Anna Harrison
- *Brand Vision* by James Everhart
- *Brand Naming* by Rob Meyerson
- *Fast Fulfillment* by Sanchoy Das
- *Multiply Your Business Value Through Brand & AI* by Rajan Narayan
- *Branding & AI* by Chahat Aggarwal
- *The Business Design Cube* by Rajagopal
- *Customer Relationship Management* by Michael Pearce
- *The Coming Age of Robots* by George Pettinico and George R. Milne
- *Market Entropy* by Rajagopal
- *Decoding Customer Value at the Bottom of the Pyramid* by Ritu Srivastava
- *Qualitative Marketing Research* by Rajagopal
- *Social Media Marketing* by Alan Charlesworth
- *Employee Ambassadorship* by Michael W Lowenstein

Concise and Applied Business Books

The Collection listed above is one of 30 business subject collections that Business Expert Press has grown to make BEP a premiere publisher of print and digital books. Our concise and applied books are for…

- Professionals and Practitioners
- Faculty who adopt our books for courses
- Librarians who know that BEP's Digital Libraries are a unique way to offer students ebooks to download, not restricted with any digital rights management
- Executive Training Course Leaders
- Business Seminar Organizers

Business Expert Press books are for anyone who needs to dig deeper on business ideas, goals, and solutions to everyday problems. Whether one print book, one ebook, or buying a digital library of 110 ebooks, we remain the affordable and smart way to be business smart. For more information, please visit www.businessexpertpress.com, or contact sales@businessexpertpress.com.

www.ingramcontent.com/pod-product-compliance
Lightning Source LLC
Chambersburg PA
CBHW061329220326
41599CB00026B/5105